Praise for THRIVE

Jim Hall emphasizes the importance of discipleship as an important function of an Acts 2 church. He not only tells us why we must disciple people, but how. This material is an excellent resource, and I encourage you to consider it as part of your training curriculum.

—Alton Garrison, assistant general superintendent of the Assemblies of God, executive director of the Division of Church Ministries and Discipleship

Jim Hall speaks from the front lines of forty years of disciple making with an authority that could only be found in the crucible of experience. *The Harvester's Handbook* [now **THRIVE**] is more than a book or a curriculum: it is a process loaded with the practical helps, powerful tools, and passionate insight that has guided hundreds of churches into the greater fruitfulness of transforming lives. Every church planter, pastor, and ministry leader will deeply benefit if they choose to follow the simple, straightforward example set forth in the highly engaging, easily multiplied message of Jim Hall's ministry found between the covers of this book.

—Dr. Tom Clegg, president and founder of the Missional Transformation Network, author of *Lost in America* and *Missing in America*

James Hall has done a great job with this very practical training manual in *The Harvester's Handbook* [now **THRIVE**]. He is right on target. Anyone wanting to learn more about personal evangelism and discipling will find it here. I heartily recommend its use.

—Dr. Robert E. Coleman, author of *The Master Plan of Evangelism*

After using your curriculum for years, I highly recommend it for discipling new converts. The materials are well thought out, easy to understand, and directly relevant to the society we live in today. I believe this is the best curriculum of its kind on the market today and has been needed in the church for years. It is self-paced and step by step with beliefs and instructions that are true for all Christians—and has made a difference in discipling our people.

—Dominic T. Gaccetta, former discipleship director for the Los Angeles Dream Center (Matthew Barnett, pastor)

I have read Jim Hall's *The Harvester's Handbook* [now **THRIVE**]. It is just what a new follower of Jesus needs. In a world where order, sequence, and truth have become like confetti blowing in the wind, this is a sequence of study that brings stability to a new believer's life.

—Bill Hull, author of *Jesus Christ, Disciplemaker* and *The Complete Book of Discipleship*

tHRIVE

DISCIPLER'S GUIDE

Mentoring new
Christians through
One PLANTs One
discipleship

JAMES H. HALL

About the author

James Hall is the son of missionaries John and Cuba Hall, with whom he spent eight and a half years growing up in Burkina Faso, West Africa. He was active in student ministries in high school and at the University of Missouri, where he received a B.A. in English literature. He earned a Master of Divinity degree from Covenant Theological Seminary in 1970. Since then he has served as Chi Alpha Director for the Illinois District Assemblies of God and as senior pastor of Urbana Assembly of God in Urbana, Illinois. After several teaching trips to Singapore, Jim and his family spent a year on the pastoral staff of Calvary Charismatic Centre (AG) in Singapore, where he began writing materials for new Christians.

Jim and his wife, Betty, have been married for forty-five years, and they have two grown children—Julie Green and Joshua. The Halls have resided in Springfield, Missouri, since 1989. After years of careful study of the Scriptures, much thought, and countless personal witnessing and discipling exchanges, God has given birth in Jim's spirit to these guidelines and lessons and helped him make them available to others. God also has called Jim to travel to churches to personally train members for personal evangelism and discipling of new believers using *THRIVE* (formerly *Harvester's Handbook*).

In March 1992 the Halls received appointment as U.S. missionaries with the Assemblies of God to focus on the major population centers of the United States to train local believers for local ministry. Their assignment has continued to encompass their ministry of training and providing materials for evangelism and discipling, but also founding and directing Urban Bible Training Centers. This program helps pastors train ministry-minded church members locally. In eighteen years, God has raised up centers in approximately forty-five cities—with as many as a thousand students enrolling at any given time.

Jim and Betty have placed approximately twelve thousand discipleship training manuals in the hands of harvest laborers across the United States. Because they have allowed photocopying of the lessons for new believers in the *THRIVE* handbook for new Christians, only in heaven will we find out how many new believers have been helped to know God with these lessons. The many testimonies received have convinced the Halls that God is in the project.

The handbook for new Christians has also been translated and distributed in Spanish, Russian, Portuguese, Bulgarian, German, and Chinese. Some translations are available as free downloads from our Web site: www.newchristian.com.

To schedule ministry or order materials, contact:

Reverend James H. Hall
16303 Audubon Village Dr
Wildwood, Missouri 63040
(636) 422-8432
E-mail: JHHalls@aol.com
Web site: www.newchristian.com (credit card orders)

Contents

Forward

Andrew heard John the Baptist speak of Jesus, and he followed Him. Then Andrew found Peter and brought him to Jesus, saying, "We have found the Messiah!" What a sequence! History has never been the same since those events. Today, believers are still finding others to bring to Jesus.

James Hall has put his knowledge, skills, and experience into creating clear, simple, but adequate guidelines for bringing people to Jesus and training them to be soul winners. He has provided a minicourse in fulfilling the great truth: "It is better to have won a soul winner, than to have won a soul to the Lord."

The dynamic principle of one-to-one discipling is set forth in clear plans in Hall's course. He has done the work for us. It puts into a pastor's or teacher's hands the principles used by Jesus in selecting His disciples and training them to go into all the world with the gospel. "Each one win one" could achieve the expectations of the evangelical world.

Dr. J. Robert Ashcroft
July 1989

Acknowledgments

First Edition (July 1989)

My Lord, whose idea this endeavor was, and who has guided and enabled its unfolding in an incredible tapestry of ways. In whatever ways **THRIVE** is helpful, the credit goes to the Lord of the harvest, while the deficiencies are the author's.

My friends in Calvary Charismatic Centre in the Republic of Singapore, who demonstrated such great devotion and diligence to disciple new believers. They presented a practical model that fired my vision to provide practical materials for disciplers anywhere and everywhere.

My wife, Betty—my best friend on the planet—who encouraged me, proofread many revisions of revisions, became "General Manager of Production," and who, along with my long-suffering children Julie and Joshua, continued to love me while I was "married" to my computer.

My parents—the ultimate "discipling friends": my father, missionary John Hall, whose Bible lesson footprints I stand in but will never fill—and who is smiling on this project from the balconies of heaven; and my mother, missionary Cuba Hall—assistant proofreader, chief intercessor, and consistent encourager—a modern example of my favorite Bible character, Barnabas.

Space does not allow comment, but I am deeply grateful for the significant parts the following individuals played in the massive team effort that these materials represent. For your encouragement and varied assistance along the way, I sincerely thank Reverend Randy Hurst; Reverend Rick Seaward; Reverend Chua Hock Lin; my "A.T.C.E.M." and "C.D.P" students in Singapore; Jim Carter; Reverend Herlin Summers; Dr. J. Robert Ashcroft; Reverend Charles Crabtree; Dr. Zenas Bicket; my sister, Evelyn Looper; and Reverend Greg White. "Your labour is not in vain in the Lord!" (1 Corinthians 15:58 KJV).

Second Edition (July 1992)

To the pastors and congregations who have desired help in leading people to Christ in addition to assistance in discipling new believers. Their enthusiasm for the teaching on evangelism and the Adoption Contract they received has encouraged me to add the section on personal evangelism to this second edition.

Their purchase of *Harvester's Handbooks* (now **THRIVE**) has made possible its availability to others.

To Reverend Robert Pirtle, Mrs. Faith Hamilton, and Reverend Charles Hackett, whose confidence and affirmation have encouraged me to seek and receive appointment as a U.S. missionary with the Assemblies of God, which has opened a wider door for the use of these materials.

Third Edition (July 2008)

Deep gratitude for this fine-tuned edition to an army of friends: To Pastors Garry Hamilton and Dave Donati and the discipling army they lead at First Assembly of God, Auburn, New Hampshire, who have demonstrated for over a decade the fruit of systematically and passionately obeying Jesus by discipling. To Dr. Leighton Jones—fellow visionary; encourager; networker; and partner in prayer, iron sharpening, and ministry. To Robert Douglas—timely encourager and ministry enlarger—another sharpener and fellow fanatic for discipling. To Phil Alessi—partner in enlarging vision and mining biblical truth, who dragged me into much needed uplifting fellowship with Church Resource Ministries (CRM). To fellow CRMers Rick Tansey and Bob Trott, who greatly helped fine tune my training strategies. To Alton Garrison, whose respect for what God has given me has expanded my platform for ministry. To Larry Pace—model lay-ministry leader, great witness in the business world, and first official fellow trainer. To Todd Waggoner, a fellow trainer whose desktopping skills and kind labors greatly enhanced the look and flow of my seminar workbook.

And in grateful memory of Carl Barnes, cofounder of Cantrell-Barnes Printing, who gave us a workable payment plan and the beginnings of twenty-one years of excellent service by CBP to help us get the Word out!

Fourth Edition—THRIVE (July 2011)

With sincere gratitude for the professional expertise in design and editing, tireless labors, provision of segments of needed content, and heart for this project of Dawn Brandon and Tammy Bicket at Between the Lines. Their assistance has truly been a godsend that will greatly increase the fruitfulness of these resources.

With heartfelt appreciation for the encouragement of Alton Garrison, Wes Bartel, and Randy Hedlun to pursue upgrading and expanding availability of these God-given resources.

Preface | Jesus' Final Command

Disciple Is a Verb

Just before Jesus returned to heaven to sit on His throne at the right hand of God the Father, He gave a command with instructions to His disciples. He also reminded them of His authority and that He would always be with them to help them—a promise of ever-present help for obedience. Read the words of Jesus from Matthew 28:18–20 (the command is in bold):

> All authority was given to Me in heaven and on earth.
> Going, therefore, **disciple all the nations**,
> Baptizing them into the name
> of the Father, and
> of the Son, and
> of the Holy Spirit,
> Teaching them to do all things that I commanded you. And look,
> I am with you all the days until the completion of the age.
> *(Matthew 28:18–20, literal rendition with author's emphasis added)*

The original word here translated as the imperative verb "disciple" is *matheteuo*. A related and more frequently used New Testament word is the Greek noun *mathetes*—commonly translated "disciple." This noun indicated learners in ancient times who accompanied their teacher in an ongoing apprenticeship-style association. *Matheteuo* is a verb with the same root as *mathetes*, meaning in this context, "to cause to learn through personal association." (A similar comparison would be to use the word *apprentice* as a verb, indicating the process used to train apprentices.) "All the nations" is the direct object of the verb—showing that this method will work and is to be used with all kinds of people at all times in all places.

Jesus had modeled what He mandated using the traditional rabbinical learning process, discipling through personal interaction with individual disciples, subgroups, and with all twelve as a team. He activated them to baptize believers, distribute miracle lunches, find transportation for His Jerusalem entrance, and make dinner preparations. He also sent them out with authority to gain ministry experience and with instructions to report back on all they did and taught.

The traditional goal of discipling was reproduction. Disciples were equipped to become rabbis who would disciple others. This was the goal of Jesus' relationship with His disciples as stated in His instructing them to teach the baptized to obey all that He had commanded them. We see specific examples of this objective being fulfilled in the early church in the discipling relationships of Barnabas with Paul; Barnabas with Mark; Barnabas and Paul with the Asia Minor believers (Acts 13); Peter with Mark; Paul with Timothy, Titus, and Priscilla and Aquila; Timothy with "faithful men" (2 Timothy 2:2); and Paul with each one of the Thessalonians (1 Thessalonians 2:11).

Personal contact was the core dynamic of this empowering process and was valued by Jesus for its natural effectiveness at imparting new convictions and new conduct to His committed followers. This personal component is evident now in mentoring, apprenticeships, and coaching relationships. To this natural process Jesus added the supernatural work of the Holy Spirit. Notice that He fully employed both natural and supernatural components.

Jesus is commanding us to do the same—to make this method the standard for dealing with all the nations. We dare not depart from or try to improve on His methods—which are effective beyond equal. As we are faithful in carrying out the Lord's prescribed methods, He will be responsible for the fruit of our labor. As we pray to the Lord of the harvest to send forth laborers, we must also be diligent to plant and water the harvest fields according to God's plan—as a farmer works in cooperation with the Creator. As we express faith by praying and enact faith by obedient works, God will give the increase of a great harvest.

The Greatness of the Great Commission

Consider the following possible scenario:

- In one year, one ready discipler wins and disciples one person to be able to win and disciple others.
- The next year, two ready disciplers each win and disciple one person to win and disciple others.
- The third year, four ready disciplers each win and disciple one person to win and disciple others.
- The fourth year, eight ready disciplers each win and disciple one person to win and disciple others.
- The fifth year, sixteen ready disciplers each win and disciple one person to win and disciple others—resulting in thirty-two discipled additions to the Kingdom from one discipling five in five years.

If this process continues—each discipled believer winning and discipling one person each year—at the end of ten years, there will be 1,023 new believers. All of this can come from a chain of obedience started by one ready discipler who disciples just ten in ten years.

The Limitations Of Involvement

The only way many new believers can be personally discipled is through the involvement of many established Christians. A few new believer follow-up specialists cannot personally disciple a multitude of new believers. A natural parallel would be something like a single mother who just gave birth to quintuplets and has no one to assist her in caring for her precious bundles. She may be called to the ministry of motherhood, but there simply is not enough of her to go around to meet the individual demands of caring for five newborns at the same time.

To neglect any of these little ones, and thus contribute to their stumbling, arouses strong feelings in the heart of their heavenly Father, elder Brother, and indwelling Helper. Yet how many new believers have spiritually died or suffered long-term from spiritual malnutrition simply from lack of individualized care to help them get a good start. A great harvest will require many church members to care for the spiritual newborns.

Conclusion

In one process, the Lord of the harvest has given us the way to raise up the best quality Christians (faithful and fruitful), who will in turn produce the greatest quantity of believers. Jesus' final command was to give ourselves wholeheartedly to this process. You hold in your hand a proven field guide—a handbook that provides practical guidelines and resources—to carry out the Great Commission in the manner commanded by the great Commissioner.

This prescribed conduct can only flow from our personal contact with the Commissioner. So the instructions in this manual begin with taking you back to Jesus to find out how He views lost people and how He feels about them. It was for their sake that He gave the Great Commission and the Holy Spirit—and put in your hands the **THRIVE** *Discipler's Guide*.

May these materials provide you with insight and guidance for teaming up with the Lord of the harvest to invest your life in One PLANTs One discipling. He has always intended for you be a fruitful witness by discipling others. In this way you will keep adding to the crowd traveling with you to where Jesus is in heaven.

Introduction

One PLANTs One Discipling

THE LORD OF THE HARVEST has earned His title by coming to earth to be the world's number-one harvester. He modeled the basic strategy and spiritual empowerment needed for the harvest (Luke 4:18). "**As** the Father has sent me, I am sending you" (John 20:21, emphasis added). He wants us to continue to proclaim His message: in His manner, with His motivation, and through His means. Much has been said about each of these critical aspects of Jesus' ministry, with the exception of His manner.

His manner was primarily defined by His personal contact with people—and ours should be as well. This does not exclude the need for other means of communication. We should communicate the gospel in any and all ways available, but at the same time, we should be diligent to keep Jesus' example of personal contact the main thing. The early church turned the world upside down with personal contact witnessing—as have believers in Latin America and China in modern times. We want to be like Jesus, and we are His church. So our ambition should be to help lost people know Jesus primarily by the way we personally relate to them.

The phases of Jesus' harvest strategy can be remembered with the acronym PLANT:

PLANT

PRAY for compassion—ask Jesus to give you His eyes and heart for lost people.

LOVE through friendship—cultivate the soil of human hearts by demonstrating the fruit of the Spirit.

ASSIST faith in Jesus—sow the seed of the gospel, and help it sprout as the lost person responds to the Spirit's convicting and drawing.

NURTURE the new believer's faith to follow Jesus—reap and retain the harvest with the Spirit's help.

TRAIN to PLANT one to PLANT another—multiply the harvest with the Spirit's power.

> The early church turned the world upside down with personal contact witnessing—as have believers in Latin America and China in modern times.

Chapter 1

Pray for Compassion

> When the Good Shepherd recovers a sheep, we can almost hear Him shouting through the hallways of heaven: "Rejoice with me; I have found my lost sheep."

Recognize how God sees people.

The ancient Eastern shepherd was not a rancher who managed large herds of livestock. He was a man who owned a small flock of sheep that he called by name and cared for individually. If one were lost, he would go search for that one until he found it and would lay it on his shoulders and take it home, rejoicing. (See Luke 15:5.)

When Jesus looked at the multitudes, He did not see a faceless crowd. He saw a great number of individuals with severe problems—all due to one cause. They were sheep separated from their shepherd (Matthew 9:36)—and He was their shepherd. Each person was created for a personal relationship with Him. Jesus also knew that the greatest tragedy, eternal hell, was in store for those who would not put their trust in Him. He wanted to rescue them and be in relationship with them—for their sakes and for His own sake—because He loved them.

For these reasons, when the Good Shepherd recovers a sheep, we can almost hear Him shouting through the hallways of heaven: "Rejoice with me; I have found my lost sheep" (Luke 15:6). All heaven celebrates when just one sheep is found.

> The depth of God's love is measured by the price He paid so runaway children can come home.

Recognize how God feels about people.

Jesus sees below the surface with people. He looks beyond the faults and the inadequate strengths and sees the root condition of people's lives—the people in the crowd were like sheep created for a shepherd's care but separated from their shepherd, harassed and helpless. Understanding this, Jesus felt compassion. And because Jesus is the accurate representation of God in human flesh, we can know how God our heavenly Father and God the Holy Spirit also feel about the lost: God feels compassion.

"God so loved the world that he gave his one and only Son" (John 3:16). To God, every world citizen is His child who has run away from home. He longs for each of them to return—though they do not deserve this privilege. The depth of His longing is measured by the price He paid to make their return possible.

Know what God is doing for people—and join Him!

God blesses the world by causing the sun to shine and the rain to fall, which causes crops to grow and produce a harvest. He gives life and meets earthly needs of people in many ways. But life on earth can only be truly good for those individuals who, like the prodigal son, return home to their heavenly Father and interact with Him in daily conversation and cooperation.

God uses this cooperation with Him to help bring other runaway children back to Him. The reconciliation He desires with the lost depends on help from the labor pool of His children who remain at home. Unfortunately, according to Jesus, the cooperation level is low: "The harvest is plentiful but the workers are few" (Matthew 9:37).

God's efforts to bring runaways home is limited by the number of human laborers actively assisting Him—and by the level of cooperation they give. He calls this joint project His harvest. It is His highest priority, but He can only pursue it as we work with Him.

To those who will join Him in loving others, He has provided His Word and His Spirit to help us be effective.

Hear what God is saying to us.

The Lord of the harvest focuses first on the labor shortage. "Ask the Lord of the harvest, therefore, to send out workers into his harvest field" (Matthew 9:38). We should pray not only for increased numbers of workers but also for increased effectiveness for those who are working. We can also make requests on behalf of specific portions of His harvest field—particular people groups (literal meaning of the Greek word translated "nations"), people in special geographical areas, and even individuals.

Remember that prayer is conversation, not just a one-way appeal for God to do something we want. As we listen, we will begin to hear from the Lord of the harvest. Now that we have shown concern for what is of greatest concern to Him, we are in a much better position to hear what our harvest supervisor has to say to us about our own personal involvement in His business. If we are truly drawing near to Him in fellowship and cooperation, we will recognize His call to join Him in befriending sinners. That's central to being like Jesus.

Jesus invites us to join Him in loving people. The good Samaritan, whom Jesus commands us to emulate, saw a man he would not naturally care for. He felt compassion for him in a way that moved him to serve the man's need sacrificially. (See Luke 10:30–37.)

Jesus knows we need help to care in that manner, so He provides to our selfish hearts His love. His indwelling Spirit delivers this love personally. The apostle Paul wrote: "God has poured out his love into our hearts by the Holy Spirit, whom he

> Being a friend to the people He is befriending is central to being like Jesus.

has given us" (Romans 5:5). This outpouring of love becomes the resource He uses to pour His love through us, manifesting itself as fruit of His Spirit (Galatians 5:22–23). This fruit causes us to care about the eternal well-being of the people we know who are on the road to hell.

If we persistently abide in Him and He abides in us, we will bear much fruit—the fruit of His Spirit living in us. It takes the supernatural work of the Spirit of adoption dwelling in us to allow us to love our neighbors as we love ourselves (Matthew 22:39). This sort of love means putting our neighbors' need for Jesus on a par with our own need for Jesus. This is well beyond the reach of whatever natural sympathy resides in us.

Go to people with God.

"We are labourers together with God" (1 Corinthians 3:9 KJV). The Spirit seeks the cooperation of the person in whom He dwells.

Combine/add your effort to His.

Our work together in the harvest becomes a combination of our natural efforts and abilities imparted by the Spirit. "Take my yoke upon you and learn from me.… For my yoke is easy and my burden is light," Jesus said (Matthew 11:29–30). Compared to the struggle of life apart from Him, truly, "his commands are not burdensome" (1 John 5:3). However, we are required to expend our natural energy as we work to do God's will.

From the New Testament, we see that working in God's harvest field may require blood and always requires sweat and tears. We must serve with the same determination as the apostle Paul and a multitude of other faithful servants. See how Paul described his effort: "We had previously suffered and been insulted in Philippi, as you know, but with the help of our God we dared to tell you his gospel in spite of strong opposition.… We loved you so much that we were delighted to share with you not only the gospel of God but our lives as well, because you had become so dear to us. Surely you remember, brothers, our toil and hardship; we worked night and day in order not to be a burden to anyone while we preached the gospel of God to you" (1 Thessalonians 2:2, 8–9).

Cooperate with the Spirit.

The harvest is already in progress. God's plan for your life is coordinated with His master plan for the harvest, with the other workers in the field, and with the stage of the work where He places you. The Lord of the harvest will give you on-the-job training and personally supervise and empower you—if your intention is to cooperate with Him. "Take my yoke upon you and learn from me," Jesus says (Matthew 11:29). We learn in the process of doing.

As you allow God to work through you, God is also working directly in the nonbeliever (John 6:44; 16:8) and through other channels. God's program in a

Our neighbors' need for Jesus will become as important to us as our own need for Jesus.

Working with Jesus in the harvest becomes a combination of our natural efforts and Spirit-imparted abilities.

nonbeliever's life is always bigger than the part you are playing (Philippians 2:13). Pray that God's whole program in a lost person's life will be effective; but you are only responsible for the part the Spirit shows you and enables you to do. Through Christ you can do all the things He wants you to do (adapted from Philippians 4:13). That is why Jesus said you are to be baptized in the Holy Spirit—so you can function as a Spirit-controlled and empowered witness (Acts 1:8).

As you allow God to work through you, God is also working directly in the nonbeliever.

Chapter 2

Love through Friendship

Don't witness to strangers.

In waiting rooms, public transportation, or fellow-traveler occasions, some kind of gesture of warmth or invitation to interaction can be extended to build a bridge for further communication. In the Western world, commonly accepted topics for casual conversation are sports, weather, a recent news item, or something humorous. This can establish an initial comfort level for more serious comments that often include current life issues that can be commented on from a God-aware perspective. If the new friend shows interest in the God factor in your conversation, proceed as led by the Spirit and the interest of the person.

The primary focus of this training, however, is the intentional building on the existing natural bridge of regular proximity with a neighbor, coworker, or acquaintance through physical fitness, recreation, or hobby activities. The associations in these venues can be viewed as divinely arranged personal harvest fields where the Lord of the harvest has placed you. Every time you participate in these activities, you are going into your world to proclaim the gospel through your conduct and your conversation. These are the components of being a witness—as empowered by the Holy Spirit according to Acts 1:8.

Connect with conversation and kindness.

The Holy Spirit will arrange these regular and one-time contacts with nonbelievers and will work in the nonbelievers' hearts to inspire interest and trust toward you. As they interact with you and sense the warmth of God's love radiating from you, they will become receptive to your message (John 4:7; Acts 8:26–31; 10:19–20). In all of your personal contacts, be warm, open, and ready to listen. Show interest in getting better acquainted by asking questions and taking time to listen. In the repeated contacts within your regular world, look for opportunities to show kindness in response to obvious needs. (This is a great and needed contrast to the combative spirit that often emanates from bold witnesses who win many arguments but few people. They often hinder the conviction the Spirit is working in the nonbeliever's heart.)

Ask questions, take time to listen, and show kindness in response to need.

Be friends.

Pursue trusted friendships with nonbelievers in your world as time goes by. Look to the Spirit to guide you as you make repeated, friendly contacts over a period of time and show practical love. Get involved socially. Look for common ground, such as conversational topics of shared interest and activities through which you can cultivate friendships. Let your friendship grow through open and honest communication without trying to appear different than what you really are. "Love your neighbor as yourself," and let your speech be "good for edification according to the need of the moment, so that it will give grace to those who hear" (Ephesians 4:29 NASB). Depend on the Holy Spirit to help you influence your friends in ways that are both natural and supernatural—and are appropriate to the stage of their journey to Jesus.

Be aware that kind deeds plow the ground of an nonbeliever's heart, helping to turn it into good soil worked for planting. Look for ways to show God's love, and opportunities to explain it. When your unbelieving friends share problems they are facing, promise to pray for God's help—even offer to pray right then. Later, inquire about the situation, assuring them that you are praying. Encourage them to pray about it too. Pray for their decisions, their families, their success, and their earthly relationships in addition to their relationship with God (1 Timothy 2:1).

This kind of interaction sends a repeated message that God cares about the details of their everyday lives and wants to have a personal relationship with them. Non-Christians usually appreciate such acts of caring. Everyone knows they need outside help. Through friendship, you will allow nonbelievers to experience Jesus in you (the fruit of the Spirit) that will help them to want their own relationship with Jesus.

Because of the self-centeredness of the human heart, non-Christians may be surprised by or suspicious of your motives. Persist patiently and peacefully, and allow the Spirit to convince them that your caring is genuine.

Trust bridges at times are built in one-time witness opportunities, as reported in the scriptural records of Jesus with the Samaritan woman and Phillip with the Ethiopian official.

Note: In your everyday encounters with nonbelievers, you can share a well-designed and clearly written gospel tract with a smile, eye contact, and a friendly "Here's some good news I'd like to give you." If the person refuses to accept, remain courteous and warm. Keep your focus on their well-being and God's love for them. And when you normally leave a tip, make it a generous—15 to 20 percent—and add a tract. Never ever leave a tract instead of a tip! (Tip + tract = missions giving.)

> Good soil has been worked for planting by kind deeds.

> When an unbelieving friend shares a problem, offer to pray right then.

Chapter 3

Assist Faith in Jesus

Speak to an audience of one.

Having built a bridge of friendship, you may now start to interactively communicate the good news as opportunities naturally occur. Lost people must have certain facts before they will entrust their lives to Jesus Christ. The most effective means of informing someone is through friendly conversation—which is, by definition, a two-way delivery system. The process goes something like this:

- Informer speaks—initiating the subject or responding to a question—and uninformed listens.
- Uninformed may ask for repetition of things not retained or for clarification where understanding was incomplete.
- Informer responds as requested, possibly reiterating or adding other information for reinforcement.
- Informer assesses level of retention and understanding by uninformed.
- Informer corrects, repeats, reinforces, or clarifies as needed—to successfully communicate and empower a healthy salvation commitment.

This is why person-to-person communication, the primary means of communicating the gospel in New Testament times, is still and always the best method of informing lost sinners of their one hope.

Know what you are trying to say.

The first step in effective communication is to have a clear understanding of the information you want to convey. For the gospel, this important information falls into two categories:

- What is new life with Jesus and its benefits? (The nonbeliever needs to know what is being recommended to awaken desire or urgency to experience Christ in his or her life.)
- How does one begin to live the new life that Jesus gives? (This information should usually be withheld until there is evidence that the person believes the gospel message.)

So let's review basic information about new life with Jesus and its benefits.

> The most effective means of informing someone is through friendly conversation—a two-way delivery system.

Understand new life with Jesus and its benefits.

The heart of the Christian life is a personal relationship with God that is like a perfect earthly relationship between a father and a child.

- The Lord's Prayer begins with the words "Our Father" (Matthew 6:9).
- John 1:12 states that we can become children of God.
- Romans 8:15–17 shows that God intends that relationship to be warm and loving ("Abba"), with two-way communication.

Every real relationship has two-way traffic—interaction of deeds, words, and feelings that travel back and forth between the two in the relationship. God loved us first and offers us a relationship. His offer of relationship is summarized in John 3:16; 1:12; and 15:14.

God offers to **forgive** our disobedience and disrespect of the holy and mighty God who created us to live by His purpose for our lives. God sent His Son, Jesus, to earth to become a man and suffer the punishment that God's justice demands for our willfulness and rebellion against God. This allows God to forgive us for breaking His rules. All we must do is agree to trust Jesus, who endured punishment for every bad thing we've done and will do. Through faith in Jesus, we are now free from the sentence of eternal death for sin, and from sin's control over our behavior. (This summarizes Jesus' role as **sacrifice** for our sins. See John 3:16.)

God offers to be our **friend**—a relationship that begins on earth and lasts forever. He comes to live inside of anyone who invites Him in, promising always to be with them. He pays attention to everything about that person and desires ongoing conversation. He also gives practical help as needed, in response to requests but often just based on the good He wants for us. Accepting His friendship means we rely on Him because He is always with us, we focus on and listen to Him, we express our love and requests to Him, and we trust Him to help us. (This summarizes Jesus' role as **Savior**. See John 1:12; 3:16.)

God offers to lead us in ways we can **follow** each day. He does this through His Word and the leading of His Spirit. He has a purpose for our whole lives, and has divided them into plans for each moment of each day through which He will personally guide us—if we pay attention to Him and obey what we understand He is telling us to do. (This summarizes Jesus' role as **Lord**. See John 15:14.)

As God's children, we receive these kinds of love from God in response to placing our faith in and dependence on Him through Jesus Christ—again described by the words *forgive*, *friend*, and *follow*. We respond to God when we…

- Ask Him for forgiveness that allows us to escape punishment and hell.
- Rely on Him as our eternal friend to provide whatever we need.
- Follow and cooperate with Him as our lead partner.

> God intends our relationship with Him to be warm and loving ("Abba"), with two-way communication.

> God's purpose for our life is divided into plans for each moment.

All this can happen only as we pay attention to Him, the one who is always with us (John 15:4–5, 14).

Pay It Forward

God's command for us to bless others ("Love your neighbor as yourself," Luke 10:27) is resourced by His blessings given to us in our relationship with Him. "Freely you have received, freely give" (Matthew 10:8).

- Receiving God's grace and forgiveness, we offer forgiveness and grace to others—we love them when they have done nothing to earn our love, or we love them in spite of their offenses against us.
- Receiving friendship from God, we offer friendship to others.
- Receiving leadership from God, we give leadership (by example and influence) to others—others can follow us and find Jesus.

We deliver these blessings to others through the natural ways that people interact—with words and actions accompanied by emotions (Luke 10:34–37; Galatians 5:22–23).

God blesses others through us with His blessing to us.

Communicate how to live new life with Jesus.

Translate the gospel into everyday life. When friends talk, they usually include some anecdotes about what has been happening in their lives or in the world around them. For the follower of Jesus, something is always happening related to Jesus. Look for opportunities to bring Jesus' activity in your life into normal conversation. Keep these discussion prompts in mind:

- For what have I asked Jesus to forgive me lately?
- How has Jesus helped me or otherwise been a friend to me lately?
- How has Jesus guided me lately?

Introduce Jesus in your life before you ask people to invite Him into theirs.

Tell the gospel clearly, in everyday language (Colossians 4:3–4). Explain the gospel in language that is guaranteed to be clear and honest to an unchurched person. Practice clear speech by writing out an explanation of the gospel—with no "Christianese." Think of an unchurched person you know, and consider his or her age, education, culture, etc. Consciously write to that person (housewife, businessman, young person, child, elderly person, etc.) using simple terms that he or she will easily and clearly understand. Remember, natural eloquence doesn't convince—only the Spirit does—so just concentrate on being clear. Use an orderly, logical development of ideas for maximum clarity and easy retention, and follow the KISS guideline—Keep It Short and Simple (but still long enough to be complete).

Avoid arguing. Be comfortable with nonbelievers' expressing disagreement with the Bible. Just aim to make clear what the Bible says (see Colossians 4:3–4), and allow the Holy Spirit to do His part of convincing that the gospel is true. The first four sessions in the *THRIVE* handbook for new Christians can be used to acquaint inquirers and seekers with the Bible's definition of a follower of Jesus.

Review the facts. Use the outline below to guide your explanation and invitation to accept Jesus and enter into a relationship for eternity, as per John 3:16; 1:12; and 15:14.

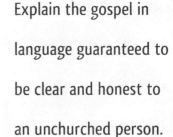

> ### Ask for and receive forgiveness from Jesus, your sin-payment (John 3:16)
>
> Review that Jesus was God in human flesh, lived a perfect life on earth, and was punished by Father God for the sins of everyone. After Jesus died, He was raised to live forever—conquering death and providing eternal life and freedom from sin's control to every person who puts his or her trust in Jesus. When a person asks for forgiveness for all disrespect of and disobedience to God, Jesus' personal suffering is counted as payment for every sin done by that person. The sentence of eternal separation from God and punishment for sin in hell is removed, and the power of sin to control that person is broken.
>
> ### Believe in and receive Jesus as your eternal friend (John 3:16; 1:12)
>
> When we invite Jesus to come live inside us as our eternal friend, our eternal relationship with God begins here on earth. Jesus, through His Spirit in us, will pay attention every moment of our life to everything about us. We can talk to Him at any time; He will talk to us; and we can depend on Him for every kind of help.
>
> ### Contract to cooperate each day with Jesus as your leader (John 15:14)
>
> When we promise to follow Jesus, it's like signing a contract to follow a new leader. We have decided to put our life under His new management, and we intend to obey the new manager. We can depend on Jesus, our eternal friend, to help us obey Him as our leader and Lord.

Explain the gospel in language guaranteed to be clear and honest to an unchurched person.

"You are my friends if you do what I command" (John 15:14 NLT).

Remove barriers. Depend on the Spirit to guide you in explaining, usually a little at a time, the content of the gospel and how to receive new life in Jesus. Each of the principles in the ABC outline explained above overcomes a common barrier presented by Satan to block faith in Christ. They include:

- "I've sinned too much for too long. God wouldn't forgive me now." Assure those who believe this that Jesus' sin payment does indeed cover all their sins—so they can ask Him to forgive them.
- "I'd like to change, but I can't. I'm in too deep." Assure people who believe this that Jesus, their friend, can and will help them make whatever changes He wants them to make. They can come to Him as they are, and He will rescue them from the prison of their sinful actions.
- "God has forgiven me and loves me as I am, so I don't need to change. I can go to heaven as I am." Be clear that being a follower of Jesus means putting one's life under new management and committing to live His way. No one reaches perfection, but we must intentionally cooperate with Jesus' leadership every day.

Trust the Spirit. As you share gospel truths in a peaceful and cheerful manner, use simple, everyday words, and trust the Holy Spirit to do the persuading. In a kindly way, you can help nonbelievers recognize and admit their need, depending on the Spirit to convince them that they have indeed offended almighty God, are separated from Him, and need forgiveness (John 16:8). Don't soft-pedal parts of the gospel truth that you think might not be acceptable to them. Remember, it's your job to communicate clearly, and it's the Holy Spirit's job to cause nonbelievers to believe that the gospel is true and to persuade them to accept God's loving offer of an eternal relationship (see Matthew 16:17).

Your friend will start to be attracted to Jesus as he or she sees and senses Jesus in you and learns about Jesus from you and from the Bible. As the person's appetite for Jesus becomes stronger and eternal issues become clearer, the nonbeliever must decide either to continue under this kind of influence or to pull back. Small decisions to continue to interact with you come from the nonbeliever's attraction to Jesus.

An eternal relationship actually begins when the nonbeliever's heart bows to the authority of Jesus. Faith in a leader is demonstrated by following, so unbelief changes to faith in Jesus as Lord when the decision is made to give up authority over one's personal life and yield to Jesus' authority.

Use ABC to guide/lead a faith-commitment prayer. When people are ready to step over the line of faith to follow Jesus, they often need assistance with this death-to-life step. Assist them as follows:

- Review the ABC truths above that define and explain how to begin an eternal relationship with God through Jesus Christ.
- Ask if they understand, believe, and agree with each segment of truth as stated. Discuss any questions or reservations they may have.

Each of the ABC provisions overcomes common barriers that block faith in Christ.

Share the gospel in a peaceful and cheerful manner, using everyday language. Trust the Holy Spirit to do the persuading.

- Explain that they need to tell God that they have decided to trust Him with their life from now on—based on their faith in Him as stated in these truths. If they are sincere, God will know it and accept their prayer. Jesus said, "Here I am! I stand at the door and knock. If anyone hears my voice and opens the door, I will come in" (Revelation 3:20).

- Encourage the convinced seekers to go ahead and talk to God in their own words. Review the ABC truths as the guide to their prayer.

- If they just can't bring themselves to pray on their own, offer to lead them in a prayer along the same lines that you encouraged them to pray—with no surprises in the prayer. Tell them to stop and discuss anything you say that they don't agree with or understand. Use words familiar to them so that they can understand immediately and easily make what you say their own prayer. Go slowly, and use short phrases, leading in a prayer that is not too brief—omitting essentials—or too long—tiring or confusing to the person following.

> **Encourage the convinced seeker to talk to God in his or her own words, using the ABC truths to guide their prayer.**

Sample Prayer

Jesus, please forgive me for all the times and ways I have disobeyed You. Jesus, please come and live inside of me and be my friend forever. Jesus, I agree to cooperate with You in the way I live my life each day. Thank You for making full payment for my sins and for loving me even though I don't deserve to be loved. Thank You also for loving me enough to help me change. I look forward to living my life with You. Amen.

After the prayer, welcome the new follower to God's eternal family as a new brother or sister. A "Happy Birthday!" is in order. Offer to begin to meet with him or her weekly to give personal help in learning to live each day in conversation and cooperation with Jesus. He or she has a great life ahead. It won't always be easy, but it will always be worth the effort.

Offer to begin to meet with your new eternal brother or sister weekly.

> **An eternal relationship begins when the nonbeliever's heart bows to the authority of Jesus.**

Conclusion

Great Expectations

You can expect God to use you when you

- pray for compassion,
- love through friendship, and
- assist people toward faith in Jesus.

Obey the inner promptings of the Spirit and take the opportunities He gives you. Work with Him to be a friend of sinners. The result will be people coming to Jesus.

Following Through

You have prepared yourself to help your friends come to Christ. You also need to prepare yourself to be a "discipling friend" to them so they will continue to follow Christ. The remainder of the **THRIVE** *Discipler's Guide* has been written to empower you to help your new brothers and sisters from this point onward. Proceed with faith and love!

Chapter 4

Nurture Faith to Follow Jesus

Welcoming New Family Members

New believers are born of the Spirit because the Spirit of adoption now lives in them, connecting them with God in a relationship with their heavenly Father. Other believers are now family members. The Holy Spirit helps new believers see and respond to God as their Father (Romans 8:15) and other Christians as brothers and sisters. God wants His family to rejoice with Him when new spiritual children are born and welcome them into His family (Luke 15:6, 9–10, 28, 32; Acts 2:41; 9:17; 11:23) He also wants the family to love them immediately as new family members. (See 1 Thessalonians 2:7–8; Luke 15:32.)

Family Nurture

Mature members of God's loving family should help His new children grow and learn to walk with God. Read in Acts 14:21–23 about Paul and Silas's (called Silvanus in some translations) discipling and coaching of new believers in Asia Minor. Read a more detailed account in 1 Thessalonians 1–2 about how Paul, Silas, and Timothy discipled the new Christians in Thessalonica (see 1 Thessalonians 2:11). These believers followed their example in turn. What did this discipling involve? We can see from Paul's example.

Paul and company…

- Prayed for new believers (1 Thessalonians 1:2–3; 3:9–13; 5:23).
- Helped them learn to walk with God (1 Thessalonians 2:7–3:13; 4:1–8; 5:10–13).
- Helped them learn to love people (1 Thessalonians 4:6–12, 18; 5:11–15).
- Rejoiced that the new believers willingly cooperated with their disciplers until they also became disciplers of new believers (1 Thessalonians 1:6–10; 2:13–14; 4:1, 9–10; 5:11).

So here are some key points to remember as you nurture new believers:

Be a discipling friend.

Spiritual growth is best served by a friendship for the purpose of discipling between a more spiritually mature brother or sister and a new believer of the same gender. They should meet at a location that is appropriately private for comfort, confidential conversation, and prayer. The new believer's kitchen table is a great

> Mature members of God's family should personally help His new children grow.

spot for this. It ensures that the believer can make the meeting and places the responsibility with the discipler for getting to the meeting consistently. The recommended frequency for meeting is once a week.

If a new believer must cancel a meeting for some reason, arrange a new time—within the same week, if possible—and resume the discussion where you left off. Be flexible with the pace of going through the sessions, adjusting to the rate at which the new believer assimilates whatever is being studied. The natural parallel is in feeding an infant: the baby decides how fast it can be fed.

Be a connecting friend.
Be the bridge to connect the new believer to the family. (See Acts 2:41–42.) Host the new family member at meetings of the church family: sit with him, introduce her, help her find the nursery, etc.

Get them talking and listening to God.
Talking to God in prayer. As new believers learn to converse directly with God in prayer, they will personally experience God's presence and power. Help new believers learn by starting with a simple and brief prayer that avoids Christian jargon or intimidating terms. Praying like this will set an example and demonstrate that prayer is simply talking with God. At some time during or at the end of discussion, encourage new believers to talk to God in their own words. Let them know that God is pleased to hear their prayer. Encourage them to talk to God frequently throughout each day.

Hearing God through the Bible and in prayer. As new believers develop the practice of talking to God frequently throughout each day, they should constantly be alert to hearing Him remind them of things they've studied in the Bible. They might hear Him speak directly to them about any thing at any time of the day. As they begin to hear God speak while praying on their own, they will be better able to recognize His voice in the middle of busy and noisy times during the day.

Get them walking and cooperating with God—obeying Him. Encourage new believers to obey whatever God shows them to do in His written Word and whatever they think God is speaking directly to them.

The Five S-sentials for Nurturing New Faith
A simple sequence of human behaviors, together with the work of the Holy Spirit, produces genuine transformation in the lives of those being discipled. The words describing each of the five phases of this transformation process all begin with the letter *S*.

1. See it.
God planned life on earth to be different from the ways people choose to live on their own. The Scriptures express what God wants us to know about Him and

---

> Be a connecting friend— the bridge that brings the new believer into his or her new church family.

> When they hear God speak while praying alone, new believers will be able to recognize His voice throughout the day.

show that He wants us to live in cooperation with Him from day to day—even moment to moment. Discipleship begins when we see what the Scriptures say about that life and how to live it and then resolve to live that way. The Bible's teaching is referred to in Scripture as "pure spiritual milk" that is essential to growing to maturity in the faith. As Peter put it: "Like newborn babies, you must crave pure spiritual milk so that you will grow into a full experience of salvation. Cry out for this nourishment, now that you have had a taste of the Lord's kindness" (1 Peter 2:2–3 NLT).

New believers need help to see for themselves what God is saying to them from the pages of His Word, and thus experience direct conversation with the God of the universe. Too often new believers are told what the Bible says but not helped to interact seriously with the text of the Scriptures for themselves. This makes God's instructions seem like secondhand truth or hearsay as opposed to direct revelation from the pages of divinely inspired writings.

2. Say it.

When disciplers discuss biblical truths with new believers, they take a critical step toward grasping these truths. Learners should be encouraged to say it—to express in their own words the information they have understood and identify what still is unclear. This gives disciplers the priceless opportunity to see the lights come on as new believers discover how eternal truth applies to earthly living. The discipler also knows when to take new believers back to the text with guiding questions and explanation until it is certain the new believer has understood—certain because the new believer has expressed the correct understanding of the passage in his or her own words.

> Disciplers know that new believers have understood when they hear them say in their own words the correct understanding of a Scripture passage.

3. Seal it.

When new believers read the Bible, they often lack confidence that they can grasp scriptural truth on their own. So when they verbalize a correct understanding of a biblical statement or concept, warmly affirm them for understanding God's truth. This will encourage them on their journey of learning and believing. Jesus did this in response to Peter's answer to the question, "Who do you say I am?" (Matthew 16:15–17). It is much easier to become "doers of the word" (James 1:22 NASB) when new believers are confident that they have heard the Word correctly.

4. Show it.

"Faith without works is dead" (James 2:26 NASB). Real faith is displayed when doing the Word follows hearing the Word. Usually, however, little accountability is demanded when the Word is taught at church. No one checks to see that believers are applying God's instructions to their lives. So is it any wonder when, without someone holding them accountable, few people complete the assignments?

> Accountability is not primarily a policing principle but rather a means of affirming and encouraging behavior changes.

One-to-one discipling allows the discipler to hold the new believer accountable for at least exerting effort to obey God's instructions. Be aware that accountability is not primarily a policing principle but rather a means of affirming and encouraging behavior changes. Correction, while included, should be done positively, with the goal of redirecting deficient behavior, rather than punitively.

A strong example of this accountability principle is found in Barnabas's relationship with the new believers in Antioch. The Bible tells us: "When he arrived and saw the evidence of the grace of God, he was glad" (Acts 11:23). Barnabas affirmed the believers for the positive change they had already experienced since conversion. Then he "encouraged them all to remain true to the Lord with all their hearts." This latter admonition parallels the commands in Hebrews 3:13 and 10:24–25 to encourage each other to increasing love and good works.

5. Share it.

This is simply repeating phases 1 through 4 (See it, Say it, Seal it, and Show it) with someone else. Jesus' mandate in Matthew 28 concludes with the instruction to teach new disciples "to obey everything I have commanded" (Matthew 28:20). It certainly would be God's intention that new believers should obey this command to disciple others, going back into the harvest field from which they just came. So the last phase of the first discipling relationship is to coach the disciple to do for others what has been done for them—by discipling someone else. This presents a great opportunity for multiplication by raising up workers for the harvest from the harvest.

Discipling Relationships

Discipling usually works best in a one-to-one relationship between an established follower and one new believer of the same gender. Modification can be made as required by your situation and the leading of the Holy Spirit. For example, if many new believers need discipling at one time, two or three can meet together with one discipler. But give each new believer individual contact outside of group meetings. Encourage friendships between the new believers in the group, but keep a watchful eye and a sensitive spirit to any hindrances to spiritual growth that might arise through these associations. Usually, such friendships will provide mutual encouragement and enhance spiritual growth. Overall, however, one-to-one discipling is recommended because it is most effective.

Make it a practice to meet once a week to discuss lesson content. In addition, be sure to make a second personal contact without a structured plan for the conversation. This second contact, in person (preferably) or by phone, should allow spontaneous interaction that will help friendship and mutual understanding to grow. Do things of common interest together to enhance your friendship and allow you to assess the new believer's spiritual growth by observing spontaneous reactions and attitudes in a variety of settings.

The last phase of discipling relationships is to coach disciples to do for others what has been done for them by discipling someone else.

Do things of common interest together to enhance your friendship and allow you to assess the new believer's spiritual growth by observing spontaneous reactions and attitudes.

Be alert to what God wants to teach you through the new believers you are helping. God always works through believers' fellowship to benefit everyone involved.

Meeting regularly is more important than completing a lesson at every meeting. The overall pace of learning should be unhurried, as it is important to give new believers whatever time is necessary to understand and apply the truth to everyday life. Often it will take two meetings to complete one lesson. Some lessons will take longer for the new believers to grasp and apply, especially if the lesson topic addresses an issue he or she struggles with. All lessons are foundational, and they are learned best when studied in the order given. The order of lessons is flexible, however, and can be adjusted to fit the needs or interests of the new believer.

How to Use the THRIVE Sessions

First Meeting

Explain to new believers that the sessions will help them learn to have their own personal relationship, including communication and cooperation, with God.

Always take time to pray together without hurry, encouraging the new believer to talk to God as simply and naturally as if talking to another person. When you pray, use simple words so the new believer can learn how easy it is to pray by listening to you. (A simple system that works well is for the discipler to begin the discussion time with prayer and for the new believer to close the time with prayer.) Pausing for brief prayers during the discussion times can be a great help to the new believer and intensify his or her awareness of God's presence as you study His Word. Such a practice models a readiness to pray at any time in the middle of regular daily activities.

Go through Session 1 with the new believer. (Refer to the Discipler Helps for assistance in guiding the new believer.) Assist in any way needed to help him or her understand how to work through the lesson (for example, how to find Bible passages if the new believer does not know how) and to understand the truth in the lesson and how it applies to everyday living. Your goal is to lead the new believer to God's written Word to hear God speak directly to him or her from the pages. The main activity of your meetings together for Session 1 should be:

- The new believer reads the questions and Bible passages out loud.
- The two of you discuss the answers.
- The new believer writes in the answers.

The discipler's own completed lessons should be brought to the meetings as notes for reference and to show the new believer that the discipler has also done the work. This will create a stronger sense of partnership between discipler and new believer in pursuing God's truth together.

Emphasize that God is more focused on their desire and effort to learn than He is on how many answers they get right the first time.

In your first meeting, also do the following:

- Explain and assign the daily time of study and prayer (quiet time) to be practiced until the next meeting between discipler and new believer.
- Arrange a regular weekly time, if possible, to meet. Be faithful in meeting with new believers—even if they are not. Their spiritual life depends on it.

Second Meeting

Go through Session 2 (or finish Session 1) with the new believer, using the same activity format as with your first meeting. Give whatever help is needed to find answers in God's Word, and discuss how those answers guide daily living. Review changes in the new believer's life, discuss his or her quiet-time experiences, and take turns praying.

Turn to the next session or session part in their edition of **THRIVE** and ask them to work through it on their own before your next meeting. Encourage new believers to give their best effort in completing the lesson but not to worry about any difficult parts. Assure them that when you meet, you will discuss and make clear the Bible's answers to the questions. Emphasize that God is more focused on their desire and effort to learn than He is on whether they get all or most of the answers right the first time.

Third Meeting

Discuss together the new believer's answers, questions, and other responses in the session assigned. Remember to regularly refer to the Discipler Helps for supportive input to your discussions with new believers. The learning activity pattern should change now to the following:

- Review application of previous lesson truths to new believer's life since last meeting.
- Read the question out loud, and ask the new believer to read the Bible passage and his or her answer to the question from the Bible passage.
- Discuss the answer until the new believer correctly understands and can write it.
- Discuss how to apply today's truth to everyday life.

Pray together. At the end of the meeting, assign the next session to be completed before the next meeting. Continue this process for the remaining lessons, referring to Discipler Helps wherever available for help with discussing each session.

General Guidelines

The first accountability issue to look for and encourage is new believers' working at the lessons on their own between meetings—and being faithful to meet for discussion. Then the focus should shift to the application of and obedience to the commands understood from Scripture and the voice of the Spirit. Also, review struggles and failures as per James 5:16; then pray together for forgiveness and successful obedience. The treasure of discipling is to see new believers' lives begin to change as they understand and obey God's Word and as they reach new levels of faith, character, and awareness of God's presence and power.

In the process of discussing the material, the discipler will see the lights come on as nuggets of truth register in the mind and heart of the new believer. To develop the disciple's responsibility to share blessings received with others, encourage him or her to share those nuggets with someone else before your next discipling meeting.

You will inevitably learn from the new believer's fresh perspective on truths you've long known. Be quick to express gratitude to the new believers for those new insights, and encourage them that God can use them to bless others. Express and reinforce from time to time the idea that discipler and disciple are simply two followers of Jesus traveling and learning together.

> The treasure of discipling is to see new believers' lives begin to change as they understand and obey God's Word.

Chapter 5

Train to PLANT Others

From New Believer to Discipler

The discipling process isn't complete until new believers reproduce themselves by becoming disciplers. During the discipling journey, begin to cast the vision for the new believer as a future discipler. Encourage the disciples to pay careful attention to what you are doing with them so that God can use them to disciple someone else as you are doing with them.

This last phase of the discipling relationship is to coach discipled new believers to obey the Great Commission by discipling someone else—using the same material and in the same manner they have been discipled. Coach the new disciplers with a monthly meeting (versus weekly, as done before)—but with the agreement that they may contact you whenever they want.

The greatest satisfaction for disciplers is when new believers you discipled become successful disciplers of other beginner believers. It is the equivalent of having spiritual grandchildren. This launches the great potential for multiplication by raising up workers *for* the harvest *from* the harvest.

Launching a Church-Based Ministry for Discipling New Believers

The challenge that comes with beginning a ministry for discipling new believers is finding existing church members willing and ready to be trained to disciple. Few were systematically and individually discipled. They will not be familiar with a one-to-one discipling relationship—and will not have experienced the impact and value of helping a new believer begin his or her walk with Jesus.

Training Discipling Friends

Training to disciple requires the experience of being discipled, so arrange a boot-camp experience to disciple your discipler trainees.

The pastor should personally recruit five to ten trusted believers who are willing to be trained as discipling friends. Thoroughly discuss phases 1 through 5 of the Guide to One PLANTs One Discipling. The main part of the training process, however, requires each trainee to independently study and write in the answers to all questions in each *THRIVE* session they'll later work through with new believers. They should look up all the Bible passages cited. Trainees should compare

> The discipling process isn't complete until new believers become disciplers.

their answers with those provided after each session, and then read and think about the Discipler Helps.

Trainees should then meet weekly as a small group, with a trainer. The trainer should facilitate discussion of the sessions, the questions, the Scripture passages referred to, the answers to the questions, and the practical application for everyday living. All participants should prepare before class and participate regularly in class discussions. Discussion will give trainees valuable practice verbalizing scriptural truth in everyday language. Most church regulars just sit and listen, never developing the ability to explain and apply biblical truths.

Group discussion should focus first on seeing the lesson content through the eyes of a new believer and discussing those truths in language anyone can understand. Refer to the Discipler Helps when discussing how to communicate to new believers. As trainees process the Scripture passages—both personally and in group discussion—God will speak new truths and reiterate, reinforce, and deepen previous insights. He will also strengthen relationships between the trainees. The result will be a mutual discipling among trainees that will produce growth, new strength, and greater understanding of the Scriptures. This will further enhance their ability to set a good example of following Christ for new believers and impart the basic skills needed to be effective discipling friends.

An option for those who desire to train as disciplers may be to choose a study partner to meet with and, together, go through the guidelines and new-believer lessons.

Conduct an ongoing evaluation of how well the discipler trainees understand and how well they communicate the lesson truths in simple language. Take care to ensure that the trainees will be good examples of sincere faith and personal behavior for new believers. (Consider: new believers' eternal lives will depend partly on the adequate preparation of those who will disciple them.) Methods of evaluation include

- personal evaluation of training-group members by the leader, based on observation and interaction inside and outside of the group's meetings (usual); or
- periodic personal interview by a qualified trainer—if the trainer has prior knowledge of the trainees' lives and walk with God (unusual).

Training of new disciplers should be considered complete only after they have assisted a new believer through all THRIVE sessions and the discipled new believer has begun to be a discipling friend to another new believer. So the "certificates" that verify new disciplers' completion of training are their disciples who become established followers of Christ and discipling friends to new believers.

Overseeing the Discipling of New Believers

The final step in the training process involves assigning new believers to the newly trained for discipling. Appoint leaders and establish a system for training

All trainees should prepare before class and participate regularly in class discussions.

Discuss Bible truths in everyday language anyone can understand.

Disciples who become established followers of Christ and discipling friends to new believers are "certificates" of successfully completed training.

disciplers and assigning new believers for discipling. Overseers of this ministry should support and hold disciplers accountable for faithful completion of the critical task of caring for new believers.

Some churches with serious discipling ministries add a nice final touch by awarding certificates in Sunday services to new believers who complete the *THRIVE* sessions with a discipler. Disciplers and the discipled give joyful testimonies of what God has accomplished in their lives. It has become a common sight in many churches for new believers receiving their certificates to reappear at numerous future recognition services alongside new believers they've discipled who are receiving their own certificates.

Note

First Assembly of God in Auburn, New Hampshire, has developed an excellent plan for organizing, training, and tracking a new-believer discipling ministry. It is available at www.newchristian.com in the Pastor's Corner, under Church Discipling Ministry. Auburn First Assembly of God—Garry Hamilton, pastor—saw more than three hundred people discipled one-to-one over a nine-year span, with many of the discipled becoming disciplers. The church sent one hundred people to help plant two new churches in recent years—and many of those were discipled and disciplers.

Summary

This Guide to One PLANTs One Discipling has shown us Jesus' strategy for gathering the harvest. The mission begins with being a friend of sinners so that we might rescue them from the fires of hell and from aimless living on earth. We must remember that Jesus is also commanding us to be discipling friends who will help new believers walk with God in daily fellowship and obedience so they will make it to heaven and bring along others they have won and discipled to win and disciple to win and…

You now have tools in your hands, understanding in your mind, and the Holy Spirit in your heart. Keep saying yes to the Lord of the harvest on this mission.

New Christian Life Materials
by James H. Hall

THRIVE

Discipler's Guide $20

- ☐ Gives complete instructions for one-to-one or small-group discipling of new Christians or for peer discipling for Christian growth
- ☐ Can be used individually for self-help instruction or for training disciplers
- ☐ New-Christian or peer discipling sessions included with answers and Discipler Helps

Handbook for New Christians $14

- ☐ Fifteen reproducible sessions for mentoring new Christians until they can win and mentor others
- ☐ Session worksheets guide new Christians to the milk of the Word, to learn how to live in daily conversation and cooperation with Jesus

Handbook for Christian Growth $15

- ☐ Fifteen sessions to facilitate growth for an individual Christian or for peer discipling teams – and also trains participants to win and mentor others
- ☐ Session worksheets guide individual Christians or peer disciplers to the written Word, to learn how to live in daily conversation and cooperation with Jesus
  (Includes assessments to identify spiritual strengths/weaknesses and spiritual gifts)

StartUp Studies.............................$3/multiples $2.50 ea.

- ☐ Four lessons adapted from Sessions 1 and 2 in the *THRIVE* handbook for new Christians, plus guidelines for evangelism/discipling by the new believer (20 pages, 8.5 in. x 5.5 in.)

To order materials and/or schedule ministry

www.newchristian.com

Rev. James H. Hall, New Christian Life Ministries
16303 Audubon Village Dr. • Wildwood, Missouri 63040
Phone: 636-422-8432 • E-mail: JHHalls@aol.com

Shipping and handling: $1.00 to $49.99—15 percent; over $50—10 percent
Make checks payable to NCLM.
Credit card orders: www.newchristian.com

Testimonies

Since your seminar, I feel so much more confident now in bringing someone to the Lord. —J.M.

Thank you for these lessons. I now recognize that God loves me and is always with me. I rest in Him now because I don't worry much. I don't think of vengeance on others. I give it all to Jesus. —I.M.

The questions can be applied on a personal level, so the believer may come to know how powerful and real our Father is. My relationship with Him has definitely changed…. My Christian friend (discipler) is great. —F.L.

We began Bible studies in homes in the projects, using the *Harvester's Handbook* [now *THRIVE*]. A number of people gave their hearts to the Lord for the first time or recommitted their lives. —G.F.

The Lord is really using this workbook to reach souls at the Kokomo Rescue Mission. It made the love of Christ so clear to me that I wanted to share it. —M.C.

At pastor/care group leader meetings, I teach a lesson, then they teach it to their care group, and then members teach it to newcomers to our church. —D.W.

People learn to read the Bible, get confidence, develop relationships, free up in worship…so many areas of their lives are affected. —S.S.

People have become bolder and more outgoing in witness and in casual meetings of persons. —R.C.

When I accepted Jesus as my Savior, I wanted to serve Him and lead a Christian life, but I didn't know how. Your lessons clearly explained how I was to live. They are a wonderful tool for new converts. Now I'll be on the teaching end. Thanks again. —C.W.

Used in hundreds of churches nationwide!
More testimonies at
www.newchristian.com

One PLANTs One

SEMINAR PARTICIPANT NOTES

Session 1

One PLANTs One Discipling

Work _____ of Jesus (Matthew 9:38; 11:29–30; John 4:37–38; 5:19).

(Each phase continues as others are launched.)

☐ 1. **P**ray for compassion for your neighbors (see and feel—John 4:35; Matthew 9:36).

☐ 2. **L**ove with Spirit fruit through friendship (_____ the soil—John 4:37–38; Matthew 13:23).

☐ 3. **A**ssist faith in Jesus (_____ seed and _____ it sprout).

☐ 4. **N**urture faith to follow Jesus (_____ the harvest).

☐ 5. **T**rain to PLANT others (_____ the harvest). All to bring in the harvest.

Personal Harvest Fields

Look at _____ Jesus has already placed in _____ harvest field. Jesus is saying: "I tell you, open your eyes and look at the fields! They are ripe for harvest" (John 4:35).

Prayerfully write names of persons in the following four fields...

- with whom you have regular speaking contact and
- who don't seem to enjoy a strong relationship with God (non-followers or new followers).

Family Field   Neighborhood Field

1. _____   1. _____

2. _____   2. _____

Employment/School Field   Recreation Field

1. _____   1. _____

2. _____   2. _____

Name one _____-Christian or _____ Christian from your fields.

Name _____   What _____ his or her faith journey?

P **PRAY for each other**. Introduce the person you named to each other, and pray for compassion in each other for those named. Pray also for God to work in the ones named.

Hear Jesus' plan for multiplying the harvest (Matthew 13:23; 28:18–20).

The Great _____ Commission: _____ all the nations (Matthew 28:19).

"I am _____ _____ always" (Matthew 28:20).

Jesus' plan is _____ to _____.

```
        ┌─────────────────┐
        │     Phase 1     │
        │                 │
        │      Going      │
        └─────────────────┘
         ↗               ↘
┌─────────────────┐   ┌─────────────────┐
│     Phase 3     │ ← │     Phase 2     │
│                 │   │                 │
│     Teaching    │   │    Baptizing    │
└─────────────────┘   └─────────────────┘
```

If you disciple to disciple, you can _____ _____ each year, or in ten years:
1+1=2+2=4+4=8+8=16+16=32+32=64+64=128+128=256+256=512+512= _____

We need to slow down to go _____.

You can't count the _____ in a _____. (See Genesis 1:11–12, 22, 28.)

Session 2

How do we work with Jesus?

_____ _____ Jesus begins to _____ (in other words, Jesus' method for _____).

table talk Describe Jesus' early public behavior. What was the message in His actions? How was Jesus training His disciples during the third and fourth passage events? (Use the space to the left for notes.)

L LOVE with Spirit fruit through friendship.

_____ the soil through:

- _____. How can conversation show compassion?

   Ask _____. _____. _____. Find out their _____ _____. Why?

   (Jesus is their _____, so what is their _____?)

- _____. Read Matthew 5:16. How can you be good news (shine _____ light) to this one?

Notes
Regarding neighbor's questions/needs:

Regarding your past/future good works:

People don't care how much you know until they know how much you care. How does your neighbor know?

ASSIST faith in Jesus. Plant _____.

Testify— _____ the gospel into everyday _____.

Each person share a "Jesus-is-my-answer" story that shows how Jesus _____ in everyday life—for example, how Jesus recently (a) forgave you, (b) helped you, or (c) guided you.

Introduce Jesus in _____ life _____ asking people to invite Him into theirs.

Clarify— _____ the gospel in everyday _____.

- _____ the _____ (character and content).

    The seed _____ a _____ with _____ all can meet— as per John 3:16, 1:12; 15:14.

    A_____ _____ from Jesus, your _____ _____ (sacrifice). (_____ "Jesus paid")

    B_____ _____ (receive) Jesus as your eternal _____ (Savior). (_____)

    C_____ to C_____ each day with Jesus as your _____ (Lord). (_____) ("In other words…" illustration: Taxi/bus)

- Make it _____ (Colossians 4:3–4).

    Assign an A, B, or C line to each table to rewrite it in language guaranteed to be _____ and _____ to an un-_____ person.

    Debrief to large group.

Use ABC to practice guiding/leading a faith commitment prayer.

Discipling in the Gospels

John 1:35–42 | When [John the Baptist] saw Jesus passing by, he said, "Look, the Lamb of God!"

When the two disciples heard him say this, they followed Jesus. Turning around, Jesus saw them following and asked, "What do you want?"

They said, "Rabbi" (which means Teacher), "where are you staying?"

"Come," he replied, "and you will see." So they went and saw where he was staying, and spent that day with him.

Mark 1:16 | As Jesus walked beside the Sea of Galilee, he saw Simon and his brother Andrew casting a net.

Mark 1:39–41 | [Jesus] traveled throughout Galilee, preaching in their synagogues and driving out demons. A man with leprosy came to him and begged him on his knees, "If you are willing, you can make me clean." Filled with compassion, Jesus reached out his hand and touched the man. "I am willing," he said. "Be clean!"

Mark 2:15 | While Jesus was having dinner at Levi's house, many tax collectors and "sinners" were eating with him and his disciples, for there were many who followed him.

Matthew 9:11–13 | When the Pharisees saw this, they asked his disciples, "Why does your teacher eat with tax collectors and 'sinners'?" On hearing this, Jesus said…. "go and learn what this means: 'I desire mercy, not sacrifice.' "

Session 3

 Watch Jesus continue to disciple.

Formal Discipling Strategies
Jesus started with non-binding **Communication**.

Then, to some, He offered a **Contract**. What were His terms?

Communication + Contract = **Coaching**

 Discuss Jesus' coaching methods described in the column on page 33. Underline key phrases.

Who and how did Jesus coach most one to one?
(Scene from *Mr. Holland's Opus*)

Describe a personal coaching/discipling experience.

Table team: Write a one-sentence definition of discipling. Share your definitions with the large group.

 Give a one-minute "teaching" to each other. Use your written definition, and illustrate with a coaching relationship in your own life.

Discipling in the Gospels

Mark 3:14 | He appointed twelve—designating them apostles—that they might be with him and that he might send them out.

Mark 4:10, 34 | When he was alone, the Twelve and the others around him asked him about the parables.... He did not say anything to them without using a parable. But when he was alone with his own disciples, he explained everything.

Mark 8:27–29 | He asked them, "Who do people say I am?" They replied, "Some say John the Baptist; others say Elijah; and still others, one of the prophets." "But what about you?" he asked. "Who do you say I am?"

Mark 6:7, 12–13, 30 | Calling the Twelve to him, he sent them out two by two and gave them authority over evil spirits.... They went out and preached that people should repent. They drove out many demons and anointed many sick people with oil and healed them.... The apostles gathered around Jesus and reported to him all they had done and taught.

Mark 8:1–2, 6–9 | During those days another large crowd gathered. Since they had nothing to eat, Jesus called his disciples to him and said, "I have compassion for these people".... He told the crowd to sit down on the ground. When he had taken the seven loaves and given thanks, he broke them and gave them to his disciples to set before the people, and they did so. They had a few small fish as well; he gave thanks for them also and told the disciples to distribute them. The people ate and were satisfied. Afterward the disciples picked up seven basketfuls of broken pieces that were left over. About four thousand men were present.

Mark 16:20 | Then the disciples went out and preached everywhere, and the Lord worked with them and confirmed his word by the signs that accompanied it.

———————————————

Matthew 14:28–31 | "Lord, if it's you," Peter replied, "tell me to come to you on the water." "Come," he said. Then Peter got down out of the boat, walked on the water and came toward Jesus. But when he saw the wind, he was afraid and, beginning to sink, cried out, "Lord, save me!" Immediately Jesus reached out his hand and caught him. "You of little faith," he said, "why did you doubt?"

Matthew 16:16–17 | Simon Peter answered, "You are the Christ, the Son of the living God." Jesus replied, "Blessed are you, Simon son of Jonah, for this was not revealed to you by man, but by my Father in heaven."

Mark 8:32–33 | Peter took him aside and began to rebuke him. But when Jesus turned and looked at his disciples, he rebuked Peter.

Luke 22:60–62 | Peter replied, "Man, I don't know what you're talking about!" Just as he was speaking, the rooster crowed. The Lord turned and looked straight at Peter. Then Peter remembered the word the Lord had spoken to him: "Before the rooster crows today, you will disown me three times." And he went outside and wept bitterly.

Mark 16:7 | Go, tell his disciples and Peter, "He is going ahead of you into Galilee. There you will see him, just as he told you."

Acts 10:13–14 | A voice told him, "Get up, Peter. Kill and eat." "Surely not, Lord!" Peter replied.

Session 4

NURTURE faith to follow Jesus. (Reaping)

After non-following friends commit to follow Jesus, they:

- _____ to be loved as a _____ _____ member. (Read 1 Thessalonians 2:7–8; Luke 15:32.)
- _____ to be coached (discipled) in learning how to _____ and _____ with Jesus. (Read 1 Thessalonians 2:11–12.)

Discipling Process: Who has the baby?
(1 Thessalonians 2:7)

The need for _____-_____-_____. A famous coach used to say: "You don't just coach a team, you coach each individual player."

1. Be a discipling _____—give _____ guidance and encouragement from the Bible. (Read 1 Thessalonians 2:11.) Meet at an _____ place and frequency (_____ _____/_____ week).

2. Be a connecting friend—assist with _____ them to the family. (Read Acts 2:41–42.)

3. Get them talking—communicating—with God.

   - Talking and listening to Him in _____—You open with a simple prayer. Have _____ close your time together with a prayer.
   - Hearing God speak through studying the _____.

4. Get them walking—cooperating—with God.

Practice Bible Study with a New Believer
Table coach: Lead a Practice Bible Study with group members who role-play as if they are a composite new believer with no church or Bible background. A guide for this

Practice Bible Study is provided at the end of these Seminar Notes. The table coach should pay close attention to the Discipler Notes.

Note: This is an exercise to help discipler trainees

(a) learn to speak clearly without using "Christianese"; and

(b) learn to help new believers discover truths from the Bible text without the discipler giving them answers. Instead, the discipler should primarily confirm the new believer's right answers as found in the Scriptures.

Five S-sentials to Nurture Faith to Follow Jesus

1. S_____ it. Help them see for themselves _____ to _____ in the Bible.

   - See why the study question is important for a new believer.
   - See the answer in the Bible text (tour guide versus storyteller).

2. S_____ it. Have them say back what _____ in their _____ words—and _____ as needed.

3. S_____ it. _____ to them when "Say it" is _____ (Matthew 16:17).

4. S_____ it. Accountability for _____ out the Word. (_____ is producing _____.)

   - _____ progress/change (Acts 11:23).
   - _____ continued growth (Hebrews 3:13; 10:24–25).

5. S_____ it. Repeat steps 1 through 4 with someone else. (Faith is producing fruit with _____.)

   - Encourage _____ sharing informally as they learn.
   - Cast _____ for discipling someone else in the future.

Session 5

TRAIN new believers to PLANT others.

New believers are _____ to multiply by _____ roles P, L, A, and N of One PLANTs One discipling. Now they are commanded to "do unto others" _____ _____ _____ _____ unto them.

Coach them as they obey the Great Connection Commission (_____ contact and _____ _____).

Being discipled isn't complete _____ new believers _____ themselves.

Big question regarding readiness to disciple: Were you ever _____ to disciple?

Conduct discipler training for the undiscipled (boot camp).

1. Recruit a training _____—or join a _____ _____ for training.

2. _____ discipling _____ _____ to disciple with the five S-sentials and the **THRIVE** Discipler's Guide.

   • Review **THRIVE** Discipler's Guide (Guide to One PLANTs One Discipling).
   • Review use of Discipler Helps and Answers in the handbook for new Christians section of the **THRIVE** Discipler's Guide.

table talk Plan the _____ and _____ of your discipler boot camp—so you can go and disciple.

Finish by asking God for faith and obedience to plant one new believer in the year ahead—and then start over again the next year as the discipled new believer does the same.

What Happened to YOU?
Guide for Practice Bible Study in Session 4

*Jesus rescued you from punishment for disobeying God
to become God's child and friend forever.*

How would you define sin?

What is God's definition of sin, based on the first sin committed?

The big question: based on this definition, are you guilty of sin?

What does your conscience say?

Let's see what the Bible says (read and fill in):

- The bad news: John 3:36 says that if you do not put your trust in (believe in) Jesus, you will not receive _____ and God's _____ will be forever on you for sinning. Did you know that sin—disobeying God—is that bad? _____ (Justice demands that someone must pay for your sins.)
- The good news: John 1:29 says God sent Jesus to remove the _____ that had come between you and God. How is He able to do that?
- Read John 3:16–17. What did God feel toward people in the world?

    What did God do as a result of how He felt?

    What does God want you to do as a result of Jesus' coming to earth?

    What does God want you to have when you believe in Him?

- Read John 1:12. If you _____ Jesus, you will become a _____ of _____. It also says that receiving is the same as _____.

    Jesus lets you know for sure.

- How can you know that Jesus has forgiven you and has actually come to stay with you? Is it because you feel good, or because of something else? What? (See Revelation 3:20.)

This exercise will help disciplers speak clearly, without "Christianese," and facilitate learning without giving the answers. Be patient, and be sure to let the new believer answer these questions.

Be sure to require the new believer to find the answers to these questions in the texts given.

Draw out as much insight as possible from the new believer. Add whatever explanation is needed here to clarify that Jesus took on himself the sentence for our crimes against Him.

Again, the discipler should avoid the temptation to provide the answer; wait for the new believer to find in the text the answers to these questions.

tHRÍVE

A HANDBOOK FOR NEW CHRISTIANS

FORMERLY THE HARVESTER'S HANDBOOK · YOUNG CHRISTIAN MANUAL

Growing with
One PLANTs One
discipleship

JAMES H. HALL

Session Summaries

Phase 1 Orientation

Making Contact

Session 1 **Starting New Life in Jesus**
God's loving plan for you is to (1) rescue you from the punishment your sins deserve and make you His child; and (2) give you new life through His indwelling Spirit and have a personal relationship and personal conversation with you.

Session 2 **Knowing God Is Always with You**
A loving relationship with God involves both contact—being alert constantly to God's presence and staying in communication with Him; and conduct—intentionally doing everything with God.

Session 3 **Worshiping God, Loving God**
According to Jesus, the first and greatest commandment is to "Love the Lord your God with all your heart and with all your soul and with all your mind" (Matthew 22:37). God wants you to worship Him and love Him in words and actions that come from your heart. Such love is a fitting response to His love for you.

Session 4 **Working with God**
Jesus said that the second greatest command was: "Love your neighbor as yourself" (Matthew 22:39). God's plan and command is for you to actively love people, in partnership with Him, responding to needs—especially people's need for salvation.

Session 5 **Your Spiritual Birth Announcement**
Water baptism announces, illustrates, and explains your conversion and the change it brings.

Phase 2 Prayerful Living (based on the Lord's Prayer)

Contact That Leads to Conduct

Session 6 **Knowing God as Your Father**
The Lord's Prayer gives us a template for praying and living that pleases God. Who you are and what your life means becomes clear when you see God as loving Father and ruling King.

Phase 3 Responsibility

❧ *Conduct through Contact* ☙

Starting New Life in Jesus

After waterskiing, Dawson Trotman was tired, but not ready to leave the water. The fun-loving founder of Navigators, an organization built to evangelize the lost and disciple Christians, climbed into a motorboat for a ride. "Daws" asked two girls in the boat if they could swim. One said no, so he sat between them, locking arms with them for greater safety. Suddenly the speeding boat made a fast turn, bounced on a wave, and sent Daws and the nonswimmer into the water. He held her head above water until the boat could circle back. Another swimmer dove into the water and helped support the struggling girl until she was hauled to safety aboard the boat. But as hands reached down to grab her rescuer's hand, Dawson Trotman sank out of sight. So died "the Navigator," giving his life to save another's—a powerful story of sacrifice that reminds us of the one who gave His life to save us all.

Because He loves us, Jesus died so that we might live.

Discipler Helps

This is the first meeting with you as the guide and the new believer as the follower. Pray much and trust hard for a good start—for you to lead well and for the new believer to have a heart that desires help in knowing God. The new believer needs to sense your genuine love and humility plus your openness to honest responses. All this will help put him or her at ease, making conversation more natural and helpful to the discipling process.

After the usual beginning small talk that allows the new believer to sense your warmth, find a quiet place—without a television playing—and start with a brief and simple prayer. (Remember, you are teaching by example.) Then do the lesson together, having the new believer read the questions aloud. Make sure he or she understands the question, and then give him or her opportunity to answer. As much as possible, lead your new believer to find the answers to the questions in the Scriptures that are given. Early, help the new believer build confidence in his or her ability to master the lessons. Don't assume any prior knowledge of the Bible. Make sure he or she can find passages in the Bible using the references given.

Dawson Trotman's life story should also remind us that a faith commitment to Christ is eternal life assurance only if it continues in a personal daily relationship with Jesus as our friend and leader. Daws encouraged believers to study and memorize God's Word to inform their relationship with its author. Many encouragers were central to the Navigators' strategy for reaping a spiritual harvest. This has made them world leaders in winning souls and keeping them through one-to-one mentoring.

These lessons are designed to take you to the Bible for foundational Christian truths. What you will read and discuss with your Christian friend will help you live a life of conversation and cooperation with Jesus. He desires an ever-closer personal relationship with you, and He wants you to want the same.

You've said yes to the new way of life provided by God the Father through the death and resurrection of His Son, Jesus Christ. May God bless the rest of your life as you constantly experience this truth: "Anyone who belongs to Christ has become a new person. The old life is gone; a new life has begun! And all of this is a gift from God, who brought us back to himself through Christ" (2 Corinthians 5:17–18 NLT).

Part 1

God's plan has always been for Jesus to rescue you from hell to be His child.

A. Jesus is able to rescue you from going to hell (eternal punishment) because He is both God and man. The following tells who Jesus is and what He has done.

1. Jesus is God. As God, He had lived in heaven since before time began. Then He was born as a baby in Israel more than two thousand years ago, at just the right time according to God's plan.

2. Everything Jesus did on earth was good. As a man He lived to help others.

3. He lived exactly as God told Him to live; His perfect life shows us what God is like.

4. The Roman ruler over Israel, Pilate, executed Jesus at the request of Jewish leaders who were jealous of Jesus because of the crowds who followed Him. They hated Jesus because He exposed their sin.

5. When He died, Jesus took God's punishment for all the things you did wrong in God's eyes (called sin). Jesus himself never sinned, so He did not deserve to be punished. But He willingly suffered your punishment so you wouldn't have to (2 Corinthians 5:21).

6. God brought Jesus back to life, and then He returned to heaven to be eternal King. He rules now over every person who believes in Him and willingly obeys Him.

7. One day He will return to rule the whole world with love, justice, and total authority.

 In the Bible, find the book called the Gospel of John, which tells about Jesus' life. You will need to read several sections of the book called John to complete this lesson.

B. Jesus came to rescue you from the punishment you deserved for rebelling against God.

1. The Bible tells us that every person is guilty of sin and deserves eternal punishment. You can read more about this in the book of John, chapter 3, verses 16–20 (John 3:16–20). Also read verse 36 of that same chapter of John (John 3:36).

    a. According to John 3:36, what will happen to every person who does not believe in Jesus Christ?

    b. What will such a nonbeliever not see or receive?

2. Before reading John 3:36, did you understand that sin—disobeying God— is that bad? What sinful things that you've done in the past still seem attractive in light of those eternal consequences?

3. When Jesus died, He was being punished for your crimes against God. According to John 3:16, why did He allow himself to be treated this way?

    In the space below, write John 3:16, using your name instead of the terms *the world* and *whoever*.

4. After thinking about these truths, how do you feel…

    a. about your sins?

    b. toward Jesus, knowing what He did for you?

    Now thank Him for what He has done for you. Say it to Him just as you would tell another person. Praying is as simple as that, and God always hears.

5. Did you…

    a. ask for forgiveness from Jesus, your sacrifice or sin payment (John 3:16)?

    b. believe in Jesus to be your friend forever—your Savior (John 1:12; 15:14)?

    c. commit to cooperate with Him daily as your leader and Lord (John 15:14)?

C. Jesus has rescued you to become God's child!

1.B.5. This is a conversion checklist. Discuss the third point (c) to make sure the new believer has a basic understanding of Jesus' lordship over everyday life. Emphasize how important it is for the new believer to be serious about giving up self-rule to follow Jesus. Explain that this is a lifelong process of learning and doing.

1.C. Illustrate the reality of hope that comes with being rescued. A drowning person who has just been rescued from a stormy sea and is lying on the deck of the lifeboat may still be full of seawater and feel exhausted. Although at that moment the person's condition may not feel greatly improved, the outlook for the future—hope—is another story!

1. To all those who receive Jesus and believe on His name, what special right does Jesus give them? Read John 1:12.

2. How does it feel, deep down, to be God's own child?

3. You can now say, "God has put His own Spirit inside of _____ to stay forever." (Read John 14:17 and fill in the blank.)

4. As a child of God, you are now in God's family with new brothers and sisters. God wants your life to be part of theirs. Like a log in a fire that burns better in the presence of other logs, your new life with God will get stronger as you spend time in the presence of your new spiritual family. That's why you should become an active part of a church that believes that the Bible is God's message to humankind.

 Jesus, fully God and fully human, was the only perfect sacrifice capable of paying the penalty for your sins. He died so that you might have a new life as a beloved child of God forever.

Part 2

God's plan for you is new life.

Read John 3:1–8.

2. Discuss the phrase *new life*, explaining that change is basic to the Christian life. Point out that if no change were needed, there would have been no need for Jesus to come to earth. He didn't pay the penalty for our sins so we would be able to continue sinning. He has given us room to grow into a new kind of person with a different way of living—His way—which is always better than our way. It could be helpful to share some of your own experiences in dealing with change in your life. Reemphasize this need for change often.

A. You have been "born again"—given a new nature by God's Spirit, who is living in you. Read about this in John 1:12–13 and 3:3–8.

1. Because of your spiritual birth, where will you one day be able to go that you would not otherwise be allowed to enter (John 3:3, 5)?

2. Spiritual birth brings spiritual life. Your new life makes it possible for you to obey your new King, something that was impossible before no matter how hard you tried to be good. Read John 8:34–36. Whose slave were you before Jesus set you free?

3. What is different about your life since you came to Jesus?

4. Explain what has happened inside of you—the difference Jesus has made. Would you call what this a miracle? Why or why not?

5. Explain to your Christian friend how you feel on the inside.

B. You are now a newborn spiritual baby who needs to grow and get to know God, your heavenly Father. Growing will always be connected to talking with God.

   1. You were born again as a result of talking with God.

      a. Somehow you began to know that the story of Jesus as told in the Bible is true. That was God speaking to your heart.

      b. Then you talked to God when you asked Him to forgive you and to be your ruler. The result was your spiritual birth on _____ (date).

   2. Your new position as God's child means you now have the privilege of personal contact with Him. A personal relationship grows with conversation—so you must continually listen to God and talk often with Him. See the Plan of Action, below, for instructions on how to do this.

   God is now your heavenly Father, and you are His child. God's Spirit is living in you, so you are always in direct personal contact with God. Being close to God this way calls for ongoing conversation with Him.

Plan of Action

God's plan for you, His child, is to grow a personal relationship with you.

1. Conversation with God is best learned by setting aside a regular time and place each day to be alone and quiet with God. Start with fifteen to twenty minutes of time when you can talk with God and allow Him to speak to you. How does Matthew 6:6 tell us we should pray? Where and what time of day will you commit to doing this?

Where: _____   Time each day: _____

2.B.2. Emphasize that our relationship with God is developed through conversation with Him. Salvation is not primarily eternal life insurance but reconciliation with God and the establishment of a loving relationship. God desires conversation, and so should we. Focus the new believer on learning to have a quiet time for communicating with God. (Note: The new believer has already been in conversation with the God of the universe, otherwise no conversion would have taken place. See Revelation 3:20.)

Explain that what moved the new believer to commit to Christ was the voice of God speaking to his or her spirit. When the new believer prayed to receive Christ, he or she was merely joining the conversation.

Summary. The term *His child* speaks of relationship. The reality of relationship is only realized where there is continuing conversation.

Plan of Action 1. Explain that quietness removes external distractions from hearing God's voice on the inside and that not being in a hurry is important to careful listening. Explain also that this kind of hearing is a whole new thing. It might come easily, or it might not—but persevere, because God has designed us to be able to hear His voice. Be prepared to work extensively with the new believer in developing a fruitful quiet time. You could never do anything more important for a young Christian!

Plan of Action 2.b–c. The new believer is asked to read all of John 1 so he or she can personally read about Jesus in the Bible. This also will encourage the new believer to read the Bible in longer thought units than the typical one- or two-verse segments, so he or she can learn to look at the big picture messages of the Scriptures. Teach the new believer always to look first at the broad view of a Bible passage and then read and study verses and paragraphs in their proper context.

Make sure the new believer has an easy-to-use version of the Bible or New Testament, such as the New International Version, New Living Translation, or New American Standard Bible.

Plan of Action 2.d. The simplest prayers that are meaningful will be the most helpful in getting the new believer started on a real prayer life and actual communication with God. Emphasize how little God cares for fancy language and how much He is pleased with sincere speech—in everyday language—that comes from the heart. To help the new believer get the idea, give a simple example of a praise prayer—something like, "Jesus, I praise You because You are God and You helped create the universe. I also praise You because You are the one who gives life to everything that is alive, including me!"

Things to Do 2. It is important to get the new believer started witnessing at the beginning of his or her Christian life. Remind him or her that having answers to various questions is not the important thing at this point, but simply telling what has happened in his or her own life. The new believer can give a simple explanation, using as a guide the information from Session 1 or a practical resource like the Adoption Contract or the Four Spiritual Laws. Help them understand that it's not necessary for them to win arguments about any points of disagreement with non-Christian friends or

2. In your daily quiet time, do the following:

a. Ask God to help you receive His message for you through what you are about to read in His Word, the Bible (John 14:26). Just pay attention to what you can understand. This is "hearing" God talk to you through the Bible.

b. Begin reading the Gospel of John. Keep studying chapter 1 until you meet your friend for Session 2. Read this same chapter each day, and notice how you see something new every time.

c. Underline the parts that speak to you strongly. Put a question mark beside the parts you don't understand. Then use the Bible-study worksheet provided with this lesson, and write the things asked for on the worksheet. For your first day studying chapter 1 of John, write down everything the author says about Jesus; then write how those things apply to you. Just do your best as you get started on this new project. Your Christian friend will help you.

d. After your study time, it's time for you to talk. In your own words, talk to God about the important things you wrote about from the chapter you studied.

- Praise God for the things about Him you read and also for what He has done for you and for the ways He is helping you each day.
- Talk to God about whatever else comes to your mind.
- Be sure to thank Him for coming to live inside of you and for bringing you new eternal life.
- Tell God how wonderful it is for you to be forgiven and to now belong to Him through Jesus.
- Ask Him to help you with the problems you are struggling with.
- You can also ask Him to help other people with their problems, no matter what those problems are. Remember that God created the whole universe, so He has enough power to do anything. He can even heal sickness or injury, so don't hesitate to ask Him to do things that are impossible for man to do. With God, nothing is impossible!

Reminder: Things to Do This Week

1. Have quiet time each day, completing your Daily Journal (see Appendix A for a reproducible journal page) during this time, until you meet your friend for Session 2 on _____ (date).

2. Tell the people you usually see from day to day about the big and wonderful change Jesus has made in your life. Don't argue or try to answer every question they may have—just tell them what has happened to you. You can use the material you've already covered in this course to help you explain it to them.

3. It's very important to make time to meet regularly with your Christian friend, who will help you understand what it means to be a Christian and pray for you every day. Also, attend the regular church meetings your friend encourages you to attend as a new Christian. Remember, a log needs other logs to burn well. Don't stay away from other Christians! You can find them at (write in church name, address, and meeting times):

family members. New believers should be encouraged just to say what has happened, saying it in a peaceful way and admitting ignorance when questions are too tough to answer because they are young in the faith. (If the person asking is really serious, the new believer should promise to investigate and then, with your help, follow through as promised.)

The most important thing for non-Christian acquaintances to see is the real impact—a noticeable change that Jesus is making—especially among those who knew the new believer best before he or she came to Jesus. But the new believer should be prepared for those at home to question whether all this change is temporary or permanent. The new believer should be patient and cheerful, trusting that God is at work in the needy hearts of skeptical family members. Opposition often comes from those who want to believe in Jesus but aren't sure He's for real. Such people will test the new believer to see if he or she has found something truly real, much like pushing on a wall to see if it is strong. The non-Christian may simply want to see the person under pressure to see if his or her reaction shows that there is indeed a real change.

Remind the new believer to refer to the outline of Session 1 or other literature provided for help in explaining what has happened to him or her.

Thinking Ahead. You, as the discipler, should do Session 2 with the new believer at the next meeting, which will be on _____.

After helping the new believer through Sessions 1 and 2, have him or her complete Session 3 independently in addition to continuing with a daily quiet time before your next meeting. Then, when you meet to reinforce the truths received and to correct or fill in information where necessary, discuss both the lesson and daily journal entries. Continue this pattern through Session 15.

Knowing God Is Always with You

Twelve-year-old Shayne didn't want to admit it even to himself, but he liked these new foster parents. His room wasn't as big as it had been at some of the other places, but this new couple asked him to call them Mom and Dad. No matter how badly Shayne acted, his foster father would always say, "Let's talk this through." And even when Shayne yelled and said unkind things, the man never lost his temper or raised his voice. He was firm and punished Shayne when he'd done wrong, but he always ended by telling the boy, "I love you, Son."

Shayne didn't dare believe it: he had been disappointed too many times before—sent back into the system when he became difficult or inconvenient. So he pushed hard and rebelled, trying to discover the limits of that love. But no matter how rough things got, he never did. "I'm not going away," Shayne's father often told him during his rages. "I'll always be here for you. Let me know when you want to talk."

In less than a year, the adoption was final. Shayne was a permanent member of his new family. But he knew he was really his father's son when he heard his calm response to a new foster sister's screams of frustration, "Let's talk this through."

You are now God's child, and you can always depend on Him to be with you.

You are now God's child, and you can always depend on Him to be with you. When you walk through life with God, you never have to worry that He won't want you or that you'll face anything that the two of you together can't handle.

"The Lord himself goes before you and will be with you; he will never leave you nor forsake you. Do not be afraid; do not be discouraged" (Deuteronomy 31:8). Can you hear Him whispering to your spirit: "I love you, Son; I love you, Daughter"?

As you spend time with your heavenly Father and talk with Him, you'll cultivate a close relationship and find yourself becoming more like Him. Today's lesson helps you understand how.

 Discipler Helps

The focus of these early lessons is to help the new believer experience God, not just know about Him. It is of utmost importance for the new believer to make and maintain real contact/interaction with God himself.

We proclaim a message of personal relationship that goes beyond simply believing the right things. Explain to the new believer that his or her personal contact with God will be similar in many ways to that of other Christians and uniquely individual in other ways.

God created and values each of us as unique beings, so His relationship with us will have characteristics that are not quite like His contact with anyone else on earth. Help the new believer learn the usual aspects of communicating and walking with God, but he or she can also expect to experience some things that are not common to every Christian.

Part 1

Being God's child means God is always with you.

A. God loves you greatly, and His Spirit in you brings His love. Find the book of Romans in your Bible, and read chapter 5, verse 5 (Romans 5:5). What does this verse say that indicates God is generous with His love?

B. God is always in personal contact with you. Because He loves you, He is with you and is always giving you His personal attention. Here are four ways in which God works to be close to you:

1. Read John 1:29. God sent Jesus to remove the _____ from between you and God.

2. Read John 6:44–45. Since you have come to Jesus, how does this statement show that God wanted contact with you before you wanted contact with Him?

1.B.3. John 6:56 seems like a difficult passage. Dealing with this passage now will show the new believer that many Bible passages that seem difficult have simple explanations if he or she will only ask.

3. God is with you because His Spirit is in you. Read John 6:56. Jesus gives life to your spirit, so He compares himself to food and drink that gives life to your body.

   a. What do you have to do with food and drink before it can give life to your body?

   b. What did you do so that Jesus can give life to your spirit?

   c. The result, in Jesus' words, is:

   d. Read John 14:17. You and Jesus can be "in" each other by His _____ being in you.

4. God knows everything about you in every area of your life, no matter how small it may seem. How does Jesus explain it in Luke 12:6–7?

C. Because God loves you as His precious child, He wants you to feel His presence. He wants you to hear Him in your spirit when He talks to you, and He wants you to respond. Read Romans 8:15–16.

1. From Romans 8:16, what is God saying to you?

   Do you know in your spirit that He is saying this to you? (Circle one.)

   Yes   No   Not sure

2. From Romans 8:15, what does God want you to say back to Him?

3. From what you have read in the Bible, what do you think God feels toward you as His child?

4. How do you feel about God?

 You are God's child, learning to recognize the closeness of your heavenly Father.

Part 2

Being with God results in doing things with God.

A. Jesus' conduct came from His contact with God the Father.

1. Read Luke 6:12–13. What did Jesus do immediately before He made the important decision of calling His disciples? What role do you think giving God His full attention all night played in Jesus' decision? What lesson can you learn for your own life from Jesus' example?

1.C. Express that God helps us experience His presence in our lives in many ways. Challenge the new believer to be alert and look for ways that God will show that He is with him or her.

1.C.3. Feelings are an important aspect of any meaningful personal relationship—and should play an important role in our relationship with God. Unhurried reading and thinking about God allows God to become more real to the new believer, which in turn enables him or her to bond more closely with God. If such awareness is low in the new believer, encourage him or her to continue believing, obeying, and communicating with God, and the feelings will come. Make sure he or she understands that right feelings are a result of—or follow—right action with God. Giving our attention to God first, as instructed in the Bible, will produce right feelings during and after our obedient actions. Feelings are important in life but cannot be trusted as a guide. Remember: right feelings follow right action with God and right attention to God.

2. This is a crucial point. Make sure the new believer understands this section as thoroughly as possible.

2. Read John 4:31–34. What was even more satisfying to Jesus than having a meal when He was physically hungry? This would mean that Jesus' greatest appetite was to do what?

3. Read John 5:17–20, 30. How did Jesus know what He should do?

4. Read John 5:17; 14:10. How was Jesus able to do what He did?

B. God's commands tell you what He wants you to do with Him.

1. When human authorities give commands, they do not personally help others carry them out. God gives commands, but He always helps you to obey. What is one of God's commands you feel you especially need His help to obey?

2. Read again John 15:4–5. Does God ever want you to try to accomplish something alone, or with only other people's help?

3. God's works can only be done if you do them along with God. For each of these miracles, describe the person's part and God's part.

   a. John 2:1–11

   b. John 6:5–13

4. Like you, God enjoys doing things with someone He loves. That someone in this lesson is you. How do you feel about doing things with God?

5. Have you had an experience such as Jesus had, as described in John 4:31–34, when you did something God wanted you to do and it made you feel good and strong on the inside? Write about it on another piece of paper, or tell your Christian friend about it.

It so important as a new believer to remember that you are always in contact with God. He is paying attention to you all the time. How much attention should you be giving Him? Do you see why it is important to spend lots of time giving God your full attention by studying His Word, praying, and listening for His voice? The more we know God, the more we will love and want to please Him. And better yet, as we get to know Him, we learn to know what He wants and how to please Him. The more contact we have with our heavenly Father, the more our conduct will be His working through us.

 God wants constant contact with you. Always remember that He is with you. Talk to God often, and always listen and obey as you do everything with Him.

Summary. Note how important is the new believer's quiet time in learning to walk with God.

Plan of Action

God's desire for you is to listen to and know His voice.

1. Following are some guidelines for listening to God speak to you.

   a. You have already heard God speak to you through the Bible and in your heart, when He made you know that He wanted you to give your life to Him. You obeyed His voice. As you listen with the desire to obey, God will talk to you many times about many things.

   b. Not every spiritual voice is God's. Evil spirits can put thoughts in your mind that make you want to do selfish things. Any thought or desire that tells you to do something that disagrees with the Bible or with what you know about God's character is either from your own natural self or from an evil spirit. Tell such thoughts and desires to leave you, because Jesus is your King, and you only agree with Him and what He says to do. Read 1 John 4:1–3, and discuss with your friend how to distinguish God's voice from other voices that seek to influence you.

2. Sometimes when you read your Bible, words will seem to come alive, jump off the page, or burn in your heart. That is God's Spirit telling you something you especially need to know at that time. Give special attention to obeying what God has said to you this way after discussing with your friend what God is saying.

3. Have daily quiet time. (Read and take notes on chapters 2 through 6 in John before the next session.)

   a. Use the Daily Journal again with this session. Each day, read a chapter in John and write about the wonderful things you see in that chapter.

   b. Review and follow the guidelines for prayer from Session 1.

Plan of Action 1.b. Inquire of the new believer regarding his or her experience in the spirit realm. Don't make a bigger issue of this than is warranted, but also don't overlook real carry-overs from involvement in the demonic spirit world that may continue to affect the new believer's life. Deal with whatever must be dealt with, and if what you encounter is beyond your experience or level of faith, ask for assistance from a more experienced and mature believer.

4. Start training yourself to speak with God often each day. He hears even your thoughts and will speak to you as you listen with your heart. You will learn to recognize certain thoughts in your mind and feelings in your heart as coming from God. God wants to speak often to you, so constantly listen for His voice. Make a practice of thanking God every hour for being with you and for all He has done for you.

5. Whenever you realize that you have acted or spoken apart from God, without giving Him your attention or without depending on Him, don't allow Satan to discourage you. Read 1 John 1:5–10. Without delay, do what verse 9 says, which is to:

What does God promise always to do in response?

6. It's important to tell others about your faith in Jesus. Read Matthew 10:16–20. When you tell someone about Jesus and how you are learning to know Him, you might notice that sometimes thoughts and words come into your mind and out of your mouth before you even know what you are saying. God helps His children say the right things when they talk to other people about Him.

 Don't forget…He is always with you, giving you His full attention! Allow your contact with God to produce good conduct with God. Train yourself to constantly listen for God's voice to help you know what to do. Then depend on His help to do it. Most of the time it will be easy. Just think, "What would Jesus do?" If God wants you to do something less obvious, ask God, "Can You and I do this together?" He will tell you what to do, so listen. And always remember, He is always with you.

Reminder: Things to Do This Week

1. Continue studying and praying daily in your quiet time. Also, work through Session 3 by yourself before your next regular meeting with your Christian friend. In addition to discussing Session 3, tell him or her about times when you hear God speak to you, what you do in response, and what happens after that. And don't forget to keep attending regular church meetings at:

2. Write a Daily Journal entry for each chapter of the Bible you read each day. Keep moving forward in your study—details are best examined after you

understand the main things. Your goal now is to see those main things. Keep in mind that God's Spirit is with you to help you understand as you put forth the effort to use the mind God gave you. Read John 14:26 and 16:13, and whenever you study, remember what Jesus promised.

Worshiping God, Loving God

The earliest known valentine is in the British Museum in London. It was sent by Charles, the Duke of Orleans, to his wife in 1415. It wasn't until the eighteenth century that sending valentines became a tradition. In their early forms, they were homemade, and the verses were composed by the sender specifically for the intended recipient.

God sent the greatest personal valentine message to all of us when "the Word became human and made his home among us" (John 1:14 NLT) "He existed in the beginning with God. God created everything through him.... The Word gave life to everything that was created, and his life brought life to everyone" (John 1:2–4 NLT). The greatest gift of love to mankind was when Jesus died on the cross for us. God gave His only Son to pay for our sins. When we accept Jesus Christ to be our personal Lord and Savior, it is an act of true worship—when our commitment comes from a heart filled with love for God in response to His love for us.

> True worship always comes from a heart filled with love.

 Read Matthew 22:25–40.

Discipler Helps

Discipler helps are not provided for Session 3. Use this space to make your own personalized discipling notes.

Part 1

 True worship requires seeing God as He really is.

 Read John 4:23–24.

A. God is love, and He gives to you His true and pure love. Read Ephesians 2:4–10.

    1. According to 1 John 4:10, 19, who started loving first, God or mankind?

    2. According to Romans 5:6–8, did God love you because you were good?

B. God is spirit (John 4:24), so His love is spiritual.

    1. Read Romans 5:5. How and where does God pour out His love for you?

    2. God's love brings change, beginning on the inside.

        a. Your heart is changed by God's Spirit loving you (Ephesians 3:14–21).

        b. Read Romans 8:15–18. You know by the Spirit telling your spirit that you are God's _____.

    3. Read Romans 8:1–3, 12–14. Your natural self (what you are apart from God's influence in your life) is often called "flesh" in the Bible. It still wants to control what you do. But you don't have to obey its desires any longer. That control is now broken, as explained in verses 1–3. If you depend each moment on God's powerful Spirit in you, He will free you from obeying your old desires and give you spiritual strength to obey God instead. Read also Romans 6:6–13. Write what you learned from these passages in Romans.

C. You can only begin to see God as He really is after you receive Him and allow Him to love you.

    1. Read John 1:12–13. Who is given the right to become children of God?

    2. Read John 6:55–57. You are allowing Jesus to love you by receiving Him into your life, just as you allow food and drink to help you when you _____ and _____.

    3. You get a true view of God when you have a personal experience with Him. Read John 9:1–7, 35–38. Notice especially verses 37 and 38. The blind man began to understand Jesus' love for him after Jesus healed him. Likewise, you can see or understand God much better after you have allowed Him to show you His love for you in specific ways. What has God done for you that helps you understand Him better?

 When you see God as He truly is, you will worship Him in the proper way (John 4:24).

Part 2

 True worship begins with expressing gratitude to God for His love that you have experienced.

 Read Luke 17:11–19.

A. Gratitude is an inner recognition of the person who has shown love.

    1. Can a person receive benefits from God without being grateful to God for what He has done? (See Luke 17:17–18; Matthew 18:27–32.)

    2. Why do you think the nine lepers and the forgiven slave were ungrateful? What was different about the one leper who returned?

    3. Which are you more like, the grateful one or the ungrateful nine?

    4. Read Psalm 136, a song of praise and thanksgiving. In your quiet time, you may wish to write your own psalm thanking God for some of the wonderful things He has done for you.

B. Saying thank you gives honor to the one who gave, in recognition of the value of the benefit received.

    1. One leper responded with true gratitude to God. How does the leper's response in Luke 17:15–16 demonstrate true worship?

2. Read Philippians 4:6 and Ephesians 5:20. What does God desire from you in response to His love for you?

 It isn't enough to feel gratitude; we must express it.

Part 3

 True worship is giving your whole self to God, loving Him with every part of you. This is the only fitting response to the ways He already loves you.

 The First Commandment
Jesus said, "'Love the Lord your God with all your heart and with all your soul and with all your mind.' This is the first and greatest commandment" (Matthew 22:37–38). This is the essence of true worship. Let's look at these areas of love and worship one by one. You worship God by loving Him with…

A. All your heart.

   1. See first how valuable you are to God.

   2. Respond by making Him the greatest treasure of your heart.

B. All your soul.

   1. See first how deeply God feels for you and to what extent He gave Himself to serve you.

   2. Respond from your soul by feeling deeply for God and devoting your energies to serving Him.

C. All your mind.

   1. See how central you are in God's thoughts.

2. Respond by filling your daily thoughts with God and making Him the most important object of your study.

D. With all your heart…soul…mind.

Think about how valuable you are to God, how deeply He cares for you, and how central you are in His thoughts. Think also about the great price God paid for you, how long God plans to continue loving you, and how close to you He has made himself.

Since God loves you that much, the right kind of response is to love Him back with all of your heart, soul, and mind. The more you understand God's love for you, the more you will love Him so deeply and completely that you will put God above everything else in your life in importance to you and in your affection and thoughts. Worshiping love responds to God as the one who is most important in all of life—now and forever (1 John 2:15–17).

 We worship God when we love and serve Him with the sum total of all our parts—our will, our emotions, and our thoughts.

Part 4

 # True worship is when your heart-love for God produces your actions.

A. With whom does a selfish heart cooperate in sinning (Ephesians 2:2–3)?

1. Read John 5:44; 8:23, 34, 38–47; 12:43; and 1 John 2:15–17. These verses show why most people do the things they do. What are some of the reasons?

2. Why does a selfish heart pretend to worship God? (Matthew 6:1–8)

3. Does God receive it?

B. God wants you to live from your heart, doing everything you do as part of your love for Him. This is worship in action.

1. Jesus set a perfect example. (See John 7:16–18; 8:26–29, 42, 50, 54–55.)

2. Read John 8:28–29. Even Jesus, the perfect Son of God, did nothing on His own but spoke just what the Father taught Him. What does this passage tell you, Jesus' disciple, about how your actions can be like His—all coming from the heart?

3. How do worshiping God, talking with God, and obeying God go together? (See John 8:29; 15:14–15.)

 Realize how important it is to God that you truly worship Him from your heart as you talk and walk with Him out of love for Him.

Plan of Action

 God's plan for you, His child, is that you love Him in return for loving you first.

1. God loved you first and is happy when you love Him in return. Loving God is a lot like loving a person. You give Him your attention, you talk with Him, you thank Him for what He does for you, and you show Him love in your actions. With God, this means willingly doing everything with Him, depending on His guidance and help. This is worship living!

2. Memorize the number-one command in Matthew 22:37, and make it your motto for the rest of your life. Pray daily to understand what to do to obey God, and ask Him to help you be able to do it.

3. Daily quiet time: Read John 7 to 11 before the next session. Remember to…

   a. Study. Write what you see in each chapter, using your Daily Journal.

   b. Pray. Continue to follow the guidelines in Session 1 and following:

   • Ask God to forgive you for the ways you have been disappointing Him by disobeying Him. Pray specifically about each time you have disappointed God.

- Thank Him for the promises you discover in His Word, saying them specifically. Tell God you are trusting Him to do what He promised, His way!
- Tell God about any struggles or problems you have, and ask Him to guide you and help you deal with them in His way.
- Ask God to heal you of any sickness or injury in your body. He may heal instantly or little by little. Sometimes God will tell you specifically what He will do if you pray and believe that He will do a certain thing. Sometimes you will pray and not know just how God will answer. You can always know that He does hear your prayer and that He will answer in the way that He chooses.
- Thank God again for coming into your life, for forgiving you, and for all the other things He has done for you recently.

Reminder: Things to Do This Week

1. Keep telling others about Jesus, encouraging them to receive Him as you did.

2. Be faithful in meeting with your friend and with your "family" in church.

3. Continue to regularly have your daily quiet time with God, using the Daily Journal system you started in Sessions 1 and 2.

4. Work through the material for Session 4 before your next meeting on:

Working with God

It has been said that following Christ means laying aside your right to choose whom to love. As Christians, we are commanded to love our neighbor as we love ourselves; to love the lovely and lovable as well as the unappealing and unlovable. That's a tall order, but we can be thankful that God does not leave us to accomplish this on our own.

"God is working in you, giving you the desire and the power to do what pleases him" (Philippians 2:13 NLT).

Did you catch that? God will work with us not only to give us the power to do what pleases Him and love others, but the desire also. You don't have to love those difficult people by yourself; but you do have to love them.

During the Revolutionary War, Peter Miller showed such love to a man who had sworn to be his enemy because of religious differences. Michael Widman spit in Miller's face whenever he came upon him, often tripped him, and was even known to punch him. But, full of the love of God, Miller responded with love and kindness.

One day Miller got word that Widman had been tried as a traitor to the Revolution and condemned to hang for his crimes. Miller walked seventy miles to plead for mercy from his old acquaintance, George Washington. General Washington was unmoved—until he learned that Widman was not Miller's friend but his worst enemy. The love of Christ that overflowed from Miller's life touched and changed George Washington's heart. It also changed Widman's. Washington pardoned him, and the former enemies walked home together, friends.

God has called you to do wonderful things for Him— things too big for you to do on your own. But they're not too big for you and God to do together.

The love of God gave Peter Miller the desire and the power to show love even to someone our human nature would tell us not to love. When we follow Jesus, He helps us to lay aside our human nature and take up His godly nature.

Will you open your life for God to use you and accomplish His work? If so, get ready to love with a love that can only come from God. We'll learn how in this session.

 Read Philippians 2:13.

Part 1

God loves people and commands you to love people with His help.

A. God loves us through His Son, the Good Shepherd (John 10:1–18, 27–30).

1. Read John 10:1–18; 27–30, where Jesus calls himself the shepherd of the sheep or the Good Shepherd. Describe what the Good Shepherd does to show His love for us, His sheep.

2. After Peter had betrayed his love for Jesus and denied Him three times, Jesus gave Peter a second chance to know His love and show it to others. Read John 21:15–17. What did Jesus tell Peter to do?

3. Read 1 John 4:21. What do you hear Jesus saying to you? How is it similar to what He told Peter?

4. Read the top two commands Jesus identified in Matthew 22:36–39. Write the first, or greatest, command in your own words.

   Write the second command in your own words.

   Read its companion verses in John 13:34 and 1 John 4:21.

   How can you love as God does? (See John 13:34; 1 John 3:16; 5:2.)

B. God's love for you fills you with love that overflows to other people (1 John 4:7–21).

1. All love begins and flows from God (1 John 4:9–10, 16, 19). You must obey the first command by loving God to keep on receiving God's love. According to John 14:20–23, what is the second component besides love?

2. You can give to others from the love you have received from God, which is obeying the second command. Copy the phrases in 1 John 4:7–12 that tell about loving others out of the love you receive from God

   Read 2 Corinthians 1:3–4, which gives a similar message about how we can share with others what God gives to us.

3. When you love your other spiritual family members this way, what does it prove? (See John 13:35 and 1 John 4:7.)

   Notice that Jesus said "*are* my disciples," not *were*. This kind of love proves that you are now connected to Jesus as His disciple. You can only love others with Jesus' kind of love if you are receiving that love yourself from Jesus through your connection with Him as His disciple. (See 1 John 3:9–18; 4:7, 12.)

4. How important is it for God's love to be flowing through you to others? (See 1 John 3:10, 14–15; Matthew 5:43–48.)

5. How can you know the right way to love your neighbor, as described in the second command (Matthew 22:39)?

6. The best way of loving yourself is to allow God to love you as you trust and obey Him. The best way of loving your neighbors as yourself is to help them receive God's _____ by…

   a. Being a channel of God's loving kindness to them.

   b. Helping them know God personally so they can receive His love directly as they trust and obey Him.

God pours His love into you so His love can overflow to others.

1.B. This is a crucial point that addresses our responsibility to share God with others and be a witness for Jesus. It merits careful studying and communication, although it isn't complicated. Share some personal experiences with your new believer to show how it works and to demonstrate that it does work. A good illustration is a bucket with an incoming water supply that overflows as long as the water keeps coming in.

Part 2

Love responds to particular needs.

A. People's needs are different and require different actions on our part to meet them. Read about the neighbor in Luke 10:29–37.

    1. List all the acts of love and mercy that are shown in the story.

    2. Review the story of the unforgiving servant in Matthew 18:27-33. What sort of mercy was needed in Matthew 18:27 and 33?

    3. Jesus came because His Father loved the world so much (John 3:16). Love cares about needs. What was the greatest need Jesus came to meet? (See John 11:25–26, 40–45; 12:44–50.)

 Stay calm. Relax. Sharing your story about what Jesus has done for you doesn't have to be scary. People can and will argue with you about what you believe, but they can't argue about what has happened to you.

B. Being a witness is responding to mankind's greatest need.

    1. When you tell your family and friends about how Jesus has changed your life, you are being a _____ about Jesus to them.

        a. Remember, you are loving your neighbors—people near you—as yourself by helping them know how to receive God's love.

        b. When you witness, tell your story peacefully, with faith that the _____ will do His part, which is to _____ _____. (See John 16:7–8.)

    2. What does 1 Peter 3:15 tell you to always be ready to do?

    3. To help you get prepared to do this, take a blank sheet of paper. Write on one side the story of how you put your faith in Jesus. Work on it until it is

2.B.1.b. The Holy Spirit is called the Advocate in John 16:7, a term your new believer might not immediately connect with the Spirit. Help him or her understand that this refers to the Holy Spirit and that He is called this because He is our Advocate—our supporter, upholder, or champion—who fights on our behalf.

clear and short. You can always add details from memory when talking, if time allows.

4. Some people are not interested in hearing about Jesus, or they will be angry or scornful toward you when you speak of Jesus. Join many Christians around the world in praying for genuine love for people whether they receive or reject you. Pray also for boldness to speak the simple message of Christ with gentleness and respect and without being restrained by fear. (Read more about this in Matthew 5:43–48 and Acts 4.)

 Think of God's heartbeat as saying, "Peo-ple/peo-ple/peo-ple" (say it aloud). Ask God to give you a heart for people full of His love and His power to show it.

Summary. Along with the new believer, put your hands over your heart and repeat aloud the sound of God's heartbeat—peo-ple/peo-ple/peo-ple. Pray together—each one of you pray-ing aloud—that God will help your heart to beat with His love for people.

Plan of Action

God's plan for you, His child, is for you to love and to share His love with others.

1. Start a list of ways to obey the top two commands (Matthew 22:37, 39). Keep the list close by as a reminder and a place to make additions as you think of them. Remember, whatever God commands you to do, He helps you to do. The key is to ask for His help and keep asking (Matthew 7:7–8). Then act in faith that He will help you do it.

Plan of Action 1. Helpful here would be some personal testi-mony of facing these commands with feelings of "impossible" and then experiencing the help and breaking of God's Spirit to bring about growing obedience and God's pleasure with your progress.

2. Daily quiet time: Study John chapters 12 through 16 before the next session.

   a. Study each chapter and write what you see, using the Daily Journal system.

   b. Continue to pray as guided previously and in whatever ways brought to mind by the notes from your study of John. Ask God to guide you and give you strength and to help you overflow with His love. Also, ask Him to lead you to people whose hearts He is already preparing and to help you say whatever He wants you to say in love.

3. Discuss with your discipling friend what you are learning from the book of John. Share how God has helped you obey as well as how you have failed to obey. He or she will celebrate with you God's pleasure in your victories and God's forgiveness for your defeats (remember 1 John 1:9). Your friend will also guide you, encourage you, and pray that God will help you to cooperate with God to produce the right attitudes and actions in your day-to-day living.

Your Spiritual Birth Announcement

The young, eager camp counselors sat around the campfire during their orientation seminar just before the start of youth camp. They went around the circle giving their names, ages, and a brief testimony. When they got to a curly-haired blond man whose thick glasses seemed to intensify the passion in his eyes, he boldly proclaimed: "My name is Larry Koski, and I'm 4 years, 3 months, and 14 days old. That was when Larry Kosinski died, Jesus took my sin away, and I was born again as Larry Koski. I followed the Lord in water baptism and have followed Him in fellowship and service for 4 years, 3 months, and 14 days."

 Discipler Helps

Be diligent in expressing the urgency of the instruction and opportunity for the new believer to be baptized. Be faithful to Jesus' Great Commission, and demonstrate a serious and diligent approach to leading new Christians into this early experience of practical submission to their Lord.

That's a pretty good illustration of water baptism. It's like a funeral service and a birthday party rolled into one. The funeral part is saying good-bye to the old, selfish you that has died with Christ. The birthday celebration is the joyful recognition of the new you—raised up to new life after being born of God into His family.

The new believer generally proclaims in simple words that he or she now belongs to Jesus. This adds verbal testimony to the message of their public act of water baptism in the name of Jesus Christ.

Baptism is usually conducted in a church building, with other believers present as representatives of the family of God as it welcomes a new brother or sister. Other public venues are common, such as swimming pools, rivers, lakes, or seashores—often with others present as well. Most churches totally immerse the baptismal candidate in water.

More important than the mode of baptism, however, is that it follows and testifies to one's personal decision to follow Jesus Christ.

When you are baptized in water, you are obeying God and being a witness.

Part 1

Water baptism is a public announcement of your new faith in Jesus.

A. Water baptism should always follow a decision to place one's faith in God through Jesus.

1. In Matthew 28:19, whom does Jesus say to baptize?

2. In Mark 16:16, whom does Jesus say qualifies for water baptism?

3. Who was baptized in the early church (Acts 2:38, 41; 8:12)?

1.A.3. The early church obeyed Jesus by making baptism an early part of discipling new believers. We must do the same in obedience to the Lord of the harvest.

B. Being baptized shows our faith in Jesus as our Savior and our new leader. Trust in a leader is demonstrated by following.

1. In Matthew 28:18–20, Jesus gives instructions regarding baptism. These instructions are (circle one) suggestions / commands.

2. When you obey Jesus, you are showing your _____ for Him (John 14:15).

3. The early Christians obeyed this command. Read about them in Acts 2:38, 41; 8:12; 9:18; 10:48; 16:33; 18:8. Will you join them in obeying this command? When?

By being baptized in water, you are announcing your faith in Jesus and showing your love for Him by obeying His command.

Part 2

2. Water baptism is a drama symbolizing justification. It is an important concept for the new believer to understand. To be as clear as possible when discussing Part 2 with the new believer, you are urgently advised to thoroughly review the material before the meeting—including rehearsing your explanation aloud to yourself or to a Christian friend.

Water baptism is an illustration of conversion.

Read Romans 6:1–7.

A. Water baptism helps us visualize the spiritual work of forgiveness. Acts 22:16 describes baptism as washing your sins away. It's like you are going under water sinful and dirty and coming up forgiven and clean.

2.A–B. As the new believer is being baptized, encourage him or her to see in his or her mind the old, natural self being left under water, now dead to sin, and the new self, created in Christ Jesus for good works, being raised out of the water alive to God.

1. The Bible word for sin that has been paid for is *justification* (being justified: Romans 5:1). The process of justification is described in Romans 6:3–7.

   a. God sees you as if _____ death was your own, because Jesus' death pays in full the debt for your sins (Romans 6:5).

   b. Because the penalty demanded by God's law has been paid by Jesus, you are no longer _____, but under grace (Romans 6:14).

   c. With your debt now paid, you are no longer condemned by God's law (Romans 8:1–2). How does that make you feel?

2. Now that you are no longer condemned by sin to eternal death, you have also been set free from sin's control of your conduct. Jesus has broken the power of sin in your life.

   a. Romans 6:6–7 says: "Our old self was crucified with him so that the body of sin might be done away with [or be rendered powerless—the actual meaning of the original language], that we should no longer be _____ to sin—because anyone who has died has been _____ from sin."

   b. Romans 6:12 says: "Do not let sin _____ in your mortal body." When sin reigns, you _____ its evil desires. (See also Romans 6:14.)

   c. The things in your own life that used to control you, but don't anymore, include:

B. According to Romans 6:4, you are raised with Jesus to _____. That means going under water as if buried—then being raised up as if resurrected with new life.

1. You are free from sin and free to _____ with Jesus (Romans 6:8).

2. Because you are now joined with Jesus, you are free to behave in a new and better way (Romans 6:4–22).

   a. New behavior is now possible for you (John 14:8–18; 15:4–17).

b. New behavior is now necessary for you (John 15:1–6).

c. Your new behavior is evidence of a relationship with the Father, as it was for Jesus (John 14:5–11).

3. You have been raised with Jesus to eternal life (Romans 6:5, 9, 22–23).

a. What will happen to your body when it is raised from death (1 Corinthians 15:3–8, 35–57)?

b. Where will you live for eternity (John 12:25–26; 14:1–3)?

> By being baptized in water, you are enacting a drama that says you have "died to sin"—sin no longer condemns you or controls you—and you have been "raised up" to live a new life of following Jesus.

Plan of Action

God's plan is for you, His child, to make a public announcement of your faith by being baptized in water.

1. The visible action of your being baptized is a statement in itself of your faith in Christ. You can make an additional strong statement when you allow God to use you to speak a few sincere words into the hearts of nonbelievers present. Your words will also bring rejoicing to your spiritual family who are welcoming you into God's kingdom. Ask God to put in your mind what He wants you to say to be a witness for Him. Don't worry about it—just pray seriously and believe that God's Spirit will give you the right words. Trust Him—and open your mouth.

2. Daily quiet time: Work through John 17 through 21 before your next session.

a. Study each chapter, using the Daily Journal system. Complete one of these studies for each chapter in John, and save them in a notebook or folder.

Plan of Action 1. Do not fail to be present for your new believer's water baptism. You play an important role in the new believer's total experience by…

1. instructing him or her in the significant truths of Session 5;

2. encouraging him or her to follow through with baptism;

3. helping with arrangements and advance orientation;

4. discussing and praying with him or her about the testimony to be given just before being baptized; and then

5. being present to join the celebration. This will be especially meaningful to the new believer. Your indifferent attitude at this would give an impression similar to that of the prodigal son's older brother (Luke 15:28–30).

b. Continue to pray as guided in Sessions 1–3 and as prompted by your studies. Make a special point today of asking God to make your water baptism a birth announcement that God will use to speak to the hearts of your unbelieving family and friends—and also that your daily behavior would continuously highlight the change Jesus can bring to a person's life. Use Matthew 5:16 as a guide for your praying.

Reminder: Things to Do This Week

1. Ask your Christian friend about making arrangements to be baptized in water. Or go ahead and talk with the pastor of the church you attend to arrange for your spiritual birth announcement.

2. In preparation for your Christ-honoring baptism, pray about and plan your testimony—as explained in points 1 and 2 of this session's Plan of Action.

3. Continue your quiet time each day, and work through Session 6 before your next meeting with your friend, which will be on:

Plan of Action 2.b. Be sure to encourage the new believer to pray along these lines, and frequently pray with him or her. Reassure the new believer that even if no family or non-Christian friends attend the baptism, their knowing that he or she was baptized is still a strong and biblical witness to them that the Holy Spirit can use in their hearts. It tells them, at the very least, that the new Christian is serious about continuing with his or her faith in Christ.

For Serious Seekers
Preview Evangelism
The "Four Before" Plan

Situations

Many Americans have heard some presentation of the good news with an appeal to receive Christ. They may feel the Holy Spirit drawing them, but they hold back because they have no practical idea of what life would be like if they committed themselves to Jesus. They resist because they don't know what they would be getting into.

Many other Americans have somewhere, at sometime, prayed a salvation prayer but failed to continue in the faith. They want to be Christians, but they need more understanding of how to live the Christian life successfully so they will not make the same mistakes as they did before. They are afraid they will fail a second time.

A Solution: Preview Evangelism—the "Four Before" Plan

1. Use Sessions 1 through 4 as a discussion guide, giving the next session to the nonbeliever to take home after each meeting. If the person would like to do the sessions *before* meeting with you, provide them accordingly.

2. After discussing Session 4, review the truths covered. Ask your friend to indicate whether he or she is ready to make a decision. If the decision is positive, proceed with the salvation prayer as taught in the Plan of Action in Session 14.

3. With rejoicing, arrange to continue meeting, now with you as the discipling friend and your new brother or sister as the new believer, to continue with Sessions 5 through 15.

Knowing God as Your Father

A daughter wrote the following message to her father:

Dad, I have always been so proud and grateful that you are my father. It makes me feel good to see how much so many people love and respect you. The older I get, and the more people I meet who have had such terrible (and yet "normal" for these days) fathers, it makes me all the more grateful for the wonderful father I have. I appreciate so much that I never had to fight the TV or sports for your attention. And I feel so blessed that you are a godly father who is always praying for our family and caring about all of us.

You have made it a natural and good thing for us kids to be able to see God as our heavenly Father, which is hard for many people. And you've always done a great job of giving us the direction and attention we need.

I'm also grateful that you are such a great husband to Mom, and although she assures me you aren't perfect, you certainly set the bar high.

I hope your grandson will appreciate your example as much as I have and that he will strive to be a godly husband and father like you one day.

I love you.

In Matthew 6:9–13 Jesus opens His model prayer with, "Our Father in heaven…." It seems it is God's plan for children to get an early understanding of what He is like from their relationship with their natural father. Tragically, in modern times many fathers have fallen short of reflecting God's character in the ways they relate to their children. This lack on the part of human fathers makes it difficult for many new believers to see God as their heavenly Father in a positive way. But God will go the extra mile to reveal himself as the Father He is to those who struggle in this way—even to those who have never known their earthly father. Psalm 68:5 tells us God is "a father to the fatherless."

Don't assume that God is just like your earthly father. If your father has reflected God's nature, be thankful. If you feel there has been a breakdown in some ways, let God show you the kind of father He really is.

Discipler Helps

Sessions 6 through 10 teach the Lord's Prayer as an outline for praying and living that pleases God.

This session can be most effective if you, the discipler, take its message into your own heart in a fresh way, renewing your own view of and response to your heavenly Father. Please study the session in advance, as if it were written primarily for you. Go through it slowly, thoroughly, and prayerfully. By following the practical instructions (Plan of Action) for yourself, you will be able to effectively assist the new believer in learning from the Lord's Prayer in a way that will lay a solid foundation for his or her lifelong prayer life.

Part 1

God wants you to see Him as your Father in heaven when you pray.

A. True love and worship require a clear view of God (John 4:22–24).

  1. God wants you to see Him and relate to Him as He is / as you think He ought to be. (Underline one.)

  2. God sees you and relates to you as you are / as you want Him to see you. (Underline one.)

  3. How is your Father in heaven like and unlike your earthly father? Keep this question in mind as you study this session. Write your answer here after you have completed the session.

Jesus gives you a guide for praying and living. It is commonly called the Lord's Prayer.

B. As your Father, God has adopted you as His beloved, eternal child.

  1. How do you feel, knowing that the one true and living God, the creator of the whole universe, is actually your own Father?

  2. Read Romans 8:14–18. Why do you think God would want you to call Him Father?

  3. How is God's father's heart shown in Matthew 10:29–31?

  4. The prayer Jesus taught in Matthew 6:9–13 shows you that God, your Father, already wants to do things for you, His child. What are those things?

5. According to Matthew 7:7–11, what is one thing you must do to receive from God?

6. What plans does God have for your future (Ephesians 2:6–7)?

C. How are you responding to your Father in heaven?

1. Have you experienced the feelings described in Romans 8:15–16 and Hebrews 4:15–16? Explain.

2. Read the promise in Romans 8:28. Everyone has been tempted at times to think that God has failed him or her in some way. Have you? Explain.

3. Jesus himself endured the greatest test of faith when He died for your sins. Feel His struggle, faith, and victory as recorded in John 16:32 and Mark 15:34.

 Your Father in heaven is patient with your faith struggles as your trust in Him as your loving, heavenly Father grows. Knowing this will add much meaning to those wonderful verses in Hebrews 2:14–18; 4:14–16. Be quick to pray the prayer in Mark 9:24.

Part 2

Your Father in heaven wants you to know His loving authority.

 Read Matthew 6:9–10, 13.

A. What words here tell of God's authority?

B. How much authority does God have, and why does He have so much? Think carefully about the passage above as well as about 1 Timothy 6:13–16 before writing your answer.

C. What feelings do you have when you recognize that your Father in heaven has this much power and authority? (Notice the feelings described in Matthew 10:28–42; Hebrews 2:14–18; 4:1–2,11–16.)

 God has, along with His great love for us, ultimate authority over the universe and all in it. As such, He is worthy of our respect and reverence.

Part 3

Your Father/King wants you to see His holy nature.

Read Matthew 6:9.

A. Real love desires real understanding. God wants you to understand His holiness, and He wants you to help others to see Him as holy. Think carefully about the following to better understand why God wants you to pray that His name would be considered hallowed, or holy.

   1. Holy means "set apart as sacred and pure."

   2. *Name* refers to the reputation of the one who bears that name—the kind of person most people think that person is.

   3. When you pray the phrase, "hallowed [holy] be your name," you are asking God to help you and other people to see God as holy and to better understand His holiness.

B. Study Revelation 4:1–11, and write the key words and phrases that describe the holiness of God in heaven.

 Prayer should usually begin with looking at God. Be careful to allow God to present the true picture of himself through His written Word and through His Spirit.

Plan of Action

God's plan for you, His child, is that you should remain connected to Him as your heavenly Father.

1. Isn't it amazing that you can come directly and personally to the King who is above every king on earth or in the spirit world and be loved and cared for directly and personally by this great King who is, in fact, your own Father forever? You can know God himself—if that is your greatest desire in life and if you stay focused on Him. Sessions 6 through 10 will take you section by section through the Lord's Prayer—a model prayer that Jesus gave to help you in the process of knowing God. Go ahead and start using the whole prayer as a guide for your praying. Before you finish these sessions, God will show you things as you pray this prayer. Ask God to really help you tune in to this study of the Lord's Prayer and to what He wants you to discover as you pray.

2. The Lord's Prayer begins with worship. See God as He is revealed in this prayer, and honor Him by praying in response to what you see.

   a. Tell Him what you see.

   b. Praise Him for who and what He is and for what He has done.

   c. Thank Him for what He has done for you.

   d. Tell Him you are honored to be able to tell others about Him.

   Here is an example of how to talk with God:

   "God, I thank You that You are not an angry and cruel tyrant who makes me shake with fear. You are my Father in heaven. You are holy, and I am sinful, but I can freely come to You because Your Son Jesus paid the penalty for my sins. I love You, Father, and I want to be a child who pleases You with my love. Help me to eagerly tell others about You so they can worship You as holy and know Your great love."

Now, you pray in your own words. God is not interested in beautiful words. Rather, He loves prayers that are simple and from your heart.

3. The following the L-O-R-D outline below is a way of remembering the sections you have studied:

    a. **L**ook at God (Matthew 6:9, 13). Worship Him at the beginning and end of your prayer.

    b. **O**rder your day His way (verse 10).

    c. **R**equest your daily supplies (verses 11–12).

    d. **D**epend on Him all day (verse 13).

Reminder: Things to Do This Week

1. Daily quiet time: Congratulations on finishing John! Now begin a study on Matthew 6:1–15, which is Jesus' teaching on prayer.

2. Continue to pray as instructed in Sessions 1 through 3, using the Lord's Prayer as an added guide.

3. Work through Session 7 before you meet your friend again on:

PRAY Guide
How to Pray for One Lost Person

A simple format to guide your praying for individual lost persons can be remembered with the word PRAY:

P **Problems** my friend is having because Jesus is not in control of his or her life:

R Ways my friend is **refusing** to trust Jesus to guide and provide for him or her:

A Things I am **asking** God to do to help my friend come to Jesus:

Y **Yes**, I will obey God in the following ways to help my friend come to Jesus:

Becoming a Citizen of Heaven

Discipler Helps

If the new believer can truly accept the truth in this session, he or she will be greatly blessed throughout life. Strongly emphasize the crucial role of the truths of this study.

It seemed that everything had fallen apart. Jesus' statements that the kingdom of heaven was at hand seemed like wishful thinking. The disciples had anticipated having lead roles in an imminent government with Jesus as King. They even competed with each other for position. Then, after getting their hopes up, it seemed that Jesus had developed a death wish, for He openly antagonized the Jewish leadership until they engineered his death at the hands of the hated Romans. How can you have a kingdom without a king? It was over.

Then the unimaginable happened. Jesus was unmistakably alive again! Now with an indestructible king, they imagined that things would go quite well. They asked, "Lord, has the time come for you to free Israel and restore our kingdom?" (Acts 1:6 NLT). Jesus' reply redirected their thinking. They were believing in the right person, but they had the wrong plan. Jesus had not launched a forced-rule kingdom but an invisible, spiritual kingdom. His kingdom is not defined by a set of rules for good behavior but rather by a person's relationship with and obedience to the King himself. God's kingdom is present wherever His will is being done on earth, reflecting the worshipful obedience He receives in heaven.

God wants children who want to obey Him and who want others to obey Him.

For Peter to take a lead role in Christ's ongoing work on earth, Jesus had to make sure Peter understood that work. Their seaside breakfast conversation (John 21) focused on Peter's personal relationship with Jesus. Three times Jesus asked, "Peter, do you love me?" Each time Peter affirmed his love, Jesus gave him a command. He ended the conversation by twice repeating to Peter: "Follow me" (John 21:19, 22). Jesus' command reiterates a theme in John's gospel as Jesus several times told His followers that if they loved Him, they would keep His commandments (John 14:15, 21, 23). True love for Jesus is evident not only by feelings of love but also by obedience. God's kingdom comes wherever believers truly follow Him in obedience to His will—both written and spoken by His Spirit.

Note: This principle is unique to the Christian faith. For example, the story is told that when Buddha was dying, his followers asked how they could best remember him. He told them that remembering him was not important: it was his teaching they should remember. But in Christianity, Jesus Christ is central. While His teaching is of great importance, without the ongoing presence of the resurrected Christ and the personal relationship that He offers to share with us, Christianity is dead and we are deluded and condemned. (The apostle Paul makes a strong case for this truth in 1 Corinthians 15.)

Jesus has called you not to a religion but to a relationship with Him. This relationship gives you a citizenship in His kingdom, where you aren't obeying impersonal laws but a personal King.

Part 1

God has a kingdom on earth now.

 Read Matthew 6:10, 13.

A. God's kingdom is where people obey the King because they love and trust Him. ("Your will be done.")

   1. Jesus said that if you _____ Him, you will do what He says (John 14:15).

   2. Obedience is also an act of _____, as stated in Romans 1:5.

      a. Obedience shows faith and trust in the authority and wisdom of the one giving the command (Romans 1:3–4).

      b. Obedience shows faith and trust that the one we're obeying will care for us (Matthew 6:11–13, 33).

B. God's kingdom comes (increases) when obedience increases.

   1. When you obey God more, His kingdom comes more through your actions.

   2. When more people become Christians, God's kingdom grows. God's kingdom grew on your spiritual birthday, which was on _____.

3. When you pray for and help others come to Jesus—or help them to obey Him more—you are helping God's kingdom come. Describe something you did recently that helped God's kingdom come a little more in this way.

 We have a role to play in advancing God's kingdom on the earth now.

Part 2

 ## Obeying God includes obeying His authorities on earth.

 Read Romans 13:1–7.

A. What are God's reasons for having earthly rulers (Romans 13:4)?

1. How does God want the following people in authority to act toward the people under their authority?

   a. Governments (Romans 13:3–4)

   b. Job supervisors/employers (Colossians 4:1)

   c. Church leaders (Hebrews 13:17)

   d. Parents (Ephesians 6:4)

   e. Husbands (Ephesians 5:25–29)

2. _____ holds earthly rulers accountable for how they act toward the people under their authority (Romans 13:6; Ephesians 6:9; Hebrews 13:17).

B. God has planned for us to show different kinds of obedience to different authorities (Romans 13:7–8).

1. Children are to _____ their parents (Ephesians 6:1–2).

2.B. Discuss in practical terms the different kinds of behavior that go with submitting to different kinds of authorities presented under point B. Compare the boundaries that each authority figure has, within which appropriate authority can be exercised. (For example, a supervisor on a job site can only instruct those under his or her authority, usually during regular work hours, and pertaining to the particular job assignment the supervisor has been delegated by superiors to oversee. The supervisor cannot give commands about the behavior at home by his or her subordinates at work.)

2. Wives are to _____ to and _____ their husbands (Ephesians 5:22–24, 33).

3. According to 1 Thessalonians 5:12–13 and Hebrews 13:7, 17–19, how should church members relate to church leaders?

4. How should employees act toward their bosses (Ephesians 6:5–7)?

5. How should citizens treat civil authorities (Romans 13:1–7; 1 Timothy 2:1–2)?

C. God blesses those who obey Him by obeying earthly authorities.

1. Write the promises of Ephesians 6:1–8.

2.C.2. This is a vital point of faith in God as the believer submits to authorities who are either non-believers or believers who seem not to care about the person under their authority. Make sure the new believer understands that God will work on his or her behalf for good.

2. If you trust God and keep an obedient spirit, God will overrule the effects of mistreatment or poor leadership that may come to you through earthly authorities. Be encouraged by reading Romans 8:28 several times.

Submission—obedience to those in authority—does not always mean we must keep silent. Rather, submission is willing cooperation with those in authority.

3. In Romans 8:28, to whom does God make the promise of all things working together for good? Are you included in this group?

4. What difficulty with authority are you struggling with now? Pray with Romans 8:28 in mind. What things in your present situation are difficult to believe that God will work together for your good?

As you willingly do what God wants you to do, it frees God's Spirit to do a work in the person in authority— even if that person is a nonbeliever. That's part of God's working things together for good.

5. Can you think of any good that God may be wanting to do in your life—to teach you, change you, or to change your circumstances—by allowing this situation in your life? Are you trusting God and obeying Him?

6. What changes do you think God wants you to make in the way you respond to that difficult authority?

7. According to Acts 4:18–20, what should you do when human authorities demand direct disobedience to God?

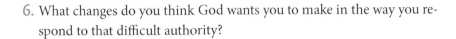

Living with the coming of God's kingdom always in your thoughts and prayers will bring glory to God and good to you. Consider the results of rebellion since Genesis 3:1–24. Live now as a citizen of God's future kingdom that will last for eternity.

Plan of Action

God's plan for you, His child, is that you should be willingly obedient.

1. The Lord's Prayer begins with worship (look at God) and continues with surrender to the will of the King (order your day His way). Use Matthew 6:10 as a guide for the second stage of your praying according to this model prayer. Here is an example:

"Lord, I want Your kingdom to come to the way I live my life today. Help me to keep paying attention to You so You can direct me and give me power to do Your will throughout this day. I especially need help with… [name any situation in which you expect to be tested that day]. May Your will be done in others' lives [name them] also." (Then pray for God's will in these people's lives—and be specific.)

2. Whose authority is difficult for you to willingly obey? Ask God to fill your heart with love for this person (remember Matthew 5:43–48) and to give you an attitude of willing obedience. (Go ahead and act with proper

obedience, as if you have the attitude of willing obedience. You will be amazed to find that the right feelings and attitudes come to you from the Lord after you take the right actions. Remember: right feelings will follow right actions.) As you, by the power of the Spirit, submit willingly to the authority as if to God, your conduct is providing God with another channel through which He can work in the life of that person. Your submission also gives God more room to work in your own life. God blesses the person who rightly obeys.

3. Daily quiet time: Continue your study of all or part of Matthew 6:1–15. Continue to pray as instructed in Sessions 1 through 3 and as prompted by your quiet time studies in Matthew 6.

 ## Reminder: Things to Do This Week

1. Continue having your quiet time each day and completing your Daily Journal. Work through Session 8 before your next meeting on:

2. Do whatever God puts in your heart from your study and prayer.

Your Daily Supply of Food

A mother shared the following testimony:

When our son Joshua was born with major heart defects, my husband and I committed him to God, confident that God loved him more than we did. After five heart surgeries, many hospital stays, and many medications, Joshua finally required open-heart surgery at age fifteen. His heart transplant at age seventeen was followed by near-fatal complications, long hospitalizations, and another serious surgery. Then he was diagnosed with non-Hodgkin's lymphoma in both lungs—a side effect of the necessary immuno-suppression medication. God brought him and us through all these crises.

Doctors had told us that we were in for a lifetime of expenses and warned us never to drop or be late with insurance-premium payments. Medical expenses accumulated against the million-dollar cap on Joshua's Blue Cross and Blue Shield insurance policy. Now we were approaching the policy's payout limit, and we knew no other company would insure him. If we lost his insurance, we would surely lose our home. Everything we earned after our tithe and living expenses went into insurance premiums and medical expenses.

One day I calculated the bills, and they came to $999,700. We were just a few hundred dollars from having no insurance for Joshua. I cried to the Lord, as I had so many times. I felt helpless surrounded by all the bills but prayed that God would help us.

That afternoon the phone rang. The woman on the other end said, "I'm calling regarding your son Joshua's insurance policy." My heart pounded, wondering if this might be the dreaded call. She said: "Blue Cross and Blue Shield's name has changed to Alliance Blue Cross and Blue Shield. The law says that if one word in a company's name changes, every policyholder's payout amount must be rolled back to zero." One little word—Alliance—had just given Joshua another million-dollar cap on his insurance policy.

God will provide for you as you worship, obey, and ask Him to "give us this day our daily bread."

Discipler Helps

This is one of the most basic and essential applications of God's kingdom come to earth. Search your own heart and make sure tithing and giving to God are areas of genuine surrender in your life—for your sake and for the sake of the new believer who is looking to you as both a model and an instructor.

I was numb, I cried, and I praised the Lord. I knew that He had been in control all the time. I have never ceased to testify to God's intervention and provision. We truly believe that if we are faithful to tithe to the Lord with what is already His, we can trust Him to meet our needs.

 Read Matthew 6:11.

Part 1

 # God is the source of provision for all of your physical needs.

 Read Psalm 23:1.

A. God is able to provide.

   1. According to Psalm 24:1, how much does God own? Whose property are you and your things (Psalm 24:1; 1 Corinthians 6:20)?

   2. Read Psalm 104. What does the writer say that shows God is able to provide for you out of what He has?

   3. Read Matthew 6:25–30 and circle the phrase that makes this sentence true: God's resource is sometimes not enough / just enough / always more than enough to meet my need. (Think of the implication of the father's statement about his possessions in Jesus' story in Luke 15:31.)

B. God wants to provide for your physical needs (Matthew 6:25–34).

   1. God always knows your need for food and clothing (Matthew 4:4; 6:11).

      a. When does He know what you need (Matthew 6:8)?

      b. Think again about what Jesus says in Matthew 6:8, 26, 32. How much do you think He knows about what you need? (See also Matthew 10:29–30.)

2. Does God promise to supply what you need or what you want (Matthew 6:19–21)?

3. When does He promise to supply: when you want to have it, or when you need it (Hebrews 4:16)?

C. You and God are partners in your life. Do your part, and you can be sure God will do His part to provide for you.

1. God wants you to _____ Him to supply what you need (Matthew 6:11; 7:7–11). Why do you think He wants you to do this?

2. What does God want you to pursue first, something that is far more important than having material things? See what Jesus says in Matthew 6:32–33.

    a. Who in this world seeks material things first (Matthew 6:32)?

    b. Why is it not necessary for you to make pursuing material things your first priority?

    c. If you put obeying God above meeting your own physical needs, should you worry that you might not have what you need? Why or why not?

 Jesus commands you not to worry about your physical needs. If you pursue first what is most important to God, He has promised to provide the essentials for your physical needs.

Part 2

Giving tithes and offerings is God's way for you to use your money to seek His kingdom first.

A. Money by itself is not valuable—we give money in exchange for what is of real value to us. What you give money for shows what is important to you.

1. Read Acts 20:33–35. Jesus said: "It is more blessed to _____ than to _____." See also Ephesians 4:28. Why is showing kindness—sharing with those in need—so important for a Christian?

2. Can your money help God's kingdom come? How?

3. Are you willing to seek God's kingdom first in the way you spend money? In Matthew 6:33, what does God promise if you do?

B. The tithe (literally a tenth: a person who tithes gives to God one tenth of his gain in money, property, crops, or animals) was an amount used in the ancient world for taxation or for honoring someone in a higher position.

1. Abraham gave a tenth of his spoils of war to honor Melchizedek (Genesis 14:16–20).

2. Jacob promised to give God a tithe if God would provide for him materially and physically (Genesis 28:10–22).

3. God commanded the nation of Israel to pay Him a tithe of all kinds of material gain (Leviticus 27:30–32). They were to give their tithe to the priests as if they were giving it to God. God instructed that some of it should be used to support the priests as well as widows, orphans, and strangers. Much of the tithe collected was used for sacrifices to God.

4. God promised His people abundant blessing if they would honor Him with their tithes by giving the full amount as worship from the heart (Malachi 1:6; 3:7–12).

   a. Sincere tithers in Old Testament times were honoring God. To withhold the tithe was to rob God of honor due Him (Malachi 1:6; 3:7–12).

   - They were honoring God as creator, supreme ruler, and owner of all the earth. This means God also owned all of "their" possessions and material gain (Psalm 24:1).

   - They were honoring God as the provider for all their physical needs (Psalm 23:1–2).

b. Tithers gained from God's hand by giving to Him, much like a farmer gains from God's increase from grain he puts in His earth (Malachi 3:10–11).

C. Offerings are voluntary gifts of goods or money to meet others' physical or spiritual needs. Gifts can be given directly to needy recipients or indirectly, through church leaders or agencies that will pass it on to those in need. This was a common demonstration of love that was commanded and practiced in the New Testament church. Both the command and the practice apply to us today as well.

1. The New Testament practice of giving is described in the following passages. Summarize in your own words what each passage says.

   a. Acts 2:44–45; 4:34–35; 20:33–35

   b. 2 Corinthians 9:1–6, 11–12

   c. Philippians 4:14–18

2. Such giving was also commanded and expected in the New Testament. Summarize in your own words the following passages.

   a. 2 Corinthians 9:6–15

   b. Galatians 6:6—giving to support church leaders and missionaries (See also Philippians 4:10–18.)

   c. Ephesians 4:28

   d. James 2:14–17

3. How is this session affecting how you see your finances?

D. God still blesses those who honor Him with material resources.

1. The best guideline for honoring God with your income is the guideline from the Old Testament of giving one tenth as a regular act of worship each

time you receive income. As an act of worship, the tenth should be given first, to show God that you want to honor Him as the first priority of your (His, actually) income. This also demonstrates faith that He will supply your needs as you give first to Him. Giving to the local church where you are under spiritual supervision and where you are regularly taught God's Word (Galatians 6:6) is similar to the Old Testament practice of giving to support the local priests as well as needy widows and other benevolence needs (Malachi 3:10).

2. God provides for Christians who give.

   a. Paul told the Philippian church that sent money for his needs: "My God will _____ all your _____" (Philippians 4:19).

   b. In 2 Corinthians 9:5–15, read Paul's words to the church that had promised a gift for struggling fellow Christians in Jerusalem. Write in your own words the main points Paul was making.

3. God also gives the giver more so she or he may continue giving to others (2 Corinthians 9:8–11).

4. According to 2 Corinthians 9:7, what kind of giver does God love?

 Good management of God's money means seeking first the kingdom of God. You do this by honoring God with a regular amount that you give as worship (the tithe principle) and giving additional offerings out of love and as God leads to help people in need. Your faith will be tested, but you will see how God will generously bless you when you give whatever He tells you to give. You can never give more than God, so obey Him in your giving of tithes and offerings.

Plan of Action

God's plan for you, His child, is that you ask Him to provide for every need as you give to Him tithes and offerings that are already His.

Receiving from God is part of your two-way relationship with Him—so it is always connected with your doing something as well. Your part in receiving God's provision of daily food is asking Him to provide and using your resources as you believe in your heart God wants you to use them. Review 2 Corinthians 9:7. Here are some steps to take to assist you in your new approach to money management:

1. Write out a simple budget to plan your regular use of income so you can be in control of your spending.

2. Include a regular amount—as often as you get paid—to give to God as worship. A tithe (one tenth of your income) is the best guideline for practicing this kind of giving as God commanded Israel to do. Pay the tithe amount first, and you will see that God makes the remaining nine tenths (if you spend it on needs and in giving to others' needs) go further than all of it did when you were managing things as if the money in your hands were actually your own.

3. List all of your basic needs and the amount needed for each thing.

4. Ask God to show you a monthly amount to give for spreading the gospel in other places.

5. Try to set aside some money for emergencies—yours or someone else's. Be alert for God's leading you to give for one-time needs (see Luke 10:33–35) Otherwise, spend only what you have budgeted. Avoid building up debt that will make you a slave to your creditors. Trust God according to the truths expressed in Philippians 4:11–13.

6. Discuss your budget with your Christian friend. Plan to report on how things are going as you and God manage His money together.

Plan of Action. Any written guideline for regular spending is an improvement over no written guideline, so encourage the new believer to do something—no matter how simple. A weekly or semimonthly review of how you are doing with your budget will be a great help in reminding the new believer to follow the budget to some degree. This may be an area of slow change, but it is vital to the new believer's spiritual growth and maturity, so persist and be encouraging.

Your Daily Supply of Forgiveness

The world was stunned one crisp October day in 2006 when Charlie Roberts parked his milk truck outside the West Nickel Mines Amish school, walked inside, and gunned down ten little girls. Five died; five were terribly wounded with point-blank gunshot wounds to the head. Horrified, people searched for a motive, but only one emerged: the gunman had not forgiven God for the death of his daughter nine years earlier. Before shooting them, he told the Amish girls, "I'm angry at God, and I need to punish some Christian girls to get even with Him."

But what happened next stunned the world even more than the tragic shooting. The Amish community forgave the murderer and reached out in compassion to his family. A father and a grandfather of two of the girls expressed forgiveness only hours after the shooting. And an Amish neighbor visited the killer's devastated parents, putting his hand on their shoulders, telling them he loved them, and comforting them for an hour. More Amish than non-Amish mourned Charlie Roberts at his funeral, and the family of one little girl invited the Roberts family to their daughter's funeral. When donations came in to help the families with funerals and medical expenses, they shared with the Roberts family.

We must follow God's example of loving those who have hurt and wronged us.

The world marveled at the forgiveness shown by the families when so greatly wronged. Roberts' family released the following statement:

"We are overwhelmed by the forgiveness, grace, and mercy that you've extended to us. Your love for our family has helped to provide the healing we so desperately need.... Your compassion has reached beyond our family, beyond our community, and is changing our world."

Forgiveness isn't easy, but we must do it. The Bible commands it, and it's the only way to heal. Those who don't forgive others hurt themselves, those they love, and everyone around them. Forgiving others as God has forgiven us not only changes us—it changes the world.

Part 1

God loves sinners—people who have wronged Him.

 Read Romans 5:8.

A. God's first step in loving you was to arrange for your forgiveness.

    1. Read Romans 5:6–8. What did God do to make it possible for Him to forgive you?

    2. God shows His willingness to forgive by loving people even before they ask Him to forgive them. What are some of the ways He shows love to people who have not asked for forgiveness (Matthew 5:45)?

    3. Before Jesus died on the cross to make it possible for every person to be forgiven, how did He show that He is a friend of sinners (Matthew 11:19; Mark 2:13–17; Luke 15:1–2)?

B. Our first step in receiving God's love is receiving His forgiveness.

    1. God cannot give you His greatest blessings until after you have accepted His forgiveness. What are these greatest blessings (John 3:16–18; Ephesians 2:1–10)?

    2. After God initially forgives you, He continues to forgive you when you stumble and sin, are sorry, and ask Him to forgive you (Matthew 6:12; 1 John 1:9). You should ask God to forgive you at least every day / week / month (circle one). (Matthew 6:11 tells you to ask God every day for the food you need.) How often do you need forgiveness?

 God loves us and forgives us in spite of our many sins against Him.

Part 2

God commands you to love those who sin against you.

 Read Matthew 6:12.

A. Why does God want you to forgive those who wrong you?

1. So you can be like your _____ (Matthew 5:43–48).

2. Because God has _____ you (Matthew 18:21–35; Ephesians 4:32; Colossians 3:13).

3. Because He has made it possible for you to forgive (Matthew 18:32–33).

B. What happens when you don't forgive those who wrong you?

1. What happens to you (Matthew 6:14–15; Hebrews 12:14–15; Ephesians 4:26–27)?

2. What happens to others around you (Hebrews 12:15)?

Forgiveness was necessary for you to come to God. Likewise, you must forgive others so you may stay with God (Matthew 6:14–15) and be healthy in your spirit (Hebrews 12:15).

 You must forgive others daily—for your own sake and for your ability to forgive others. God will freely forgive you if you ask often and forgive often.

Plan of Action

God's plan for you, His child, is for you to forgive those who have wronged you—as He has forgiven you for your sin.

 A definition of forgiveness: to set aside an offense without any demand for
  • revenge against your offender—getting even; or
  • compensation from the offender—"you owe me."

Forgiveness requires loving people in spite of their wrongs against you. You must forgive whoever sins against you if you want to receive forgiveness from God (Matthew 6:15). Following are some helpful steps:

1. On a separate piece of paper, write the names of people you still have not forgiven and how they have wronged you.

2. Ask God to help you until you can decide to forgive them. Say each name and offense before God, committing to forgive each one.

3. Ask God to help you see those people's value in God's sight—to see them as precious to God and therefore precious to you. Remember their good points. Refuse to see them as entirely bad because of their offense. Remember, you are not entirely good either.

4. Remember how much God has forgiven—and continues to forgive—you. Picture yourself standing at the foot of the cross with that person with both of you receiving forgiveness through the death and love of Jesus.

5. To represent your release of these offenses and your desire for revenge or compensation, tear up or burn your list. Thank God that He has set you free to forgive—free from the prison of bitterness. Receive your freedom by faith!

6. Recognize that feelings of hurt and resentment are normal human reactions when people wrong us. Having these feelings is no more sinful than were Jesus' temptations in the desert—what you do with those feelings is what determines if you're doing right or wrong. The first step in surrendering such feelings to God is to own them. Admit to God that these particular feelings are indeed present and active in you. Or, you may need to ask or allow God to bring to the surface feelings you have been trying to ignore. These feelings often stop us from forgiving until we admit them and give them to God. You can proceed in faith knowing that God will not allow more feelings to surface than you can handle with His help (see 1 Corinthians 10:13). Whenever you recognize these negative feelings, you should confess your feelings to God and ask Him to forgive you for holding on to them. Then ask God to heal you from the wounds they have caused you.

7. Now begin praying that God will replace those feelings of hurt and resentment with the appropriate fruit of the Spirit needed to replace them—the healthy emotions supplied by the Spirit—much like healthy tissue that replaces diseased tissue when physical healing takes place. As a prayer re-

minder, put in writing the natural feelings you want to give up in exchange for the fruit of the Spirit—feelings you want to receive. Remember, these Spirit-supplied feelings will include recognizing how valuable your offenders are in God's sight as well as positive feelings of love toward them.

This does not mean that you will regard differently what they have done. When Jesus forgives us, He does not redefine our sin or pretend we are suddenly immune to sin. Real forgiveness is offered in response to real sin. Forgiveness also does not mean that you are suddenly able to fully trust the person in the area where he or she wronged you. Trust must be rebuilt in stages: a measure of risk is taken to extend a measure of trust. As each measure of trust is rewarded by faithfulness at that level, more trust can be extended. But the forgiver must risk trust beyond the level of faithfulness demonstrated by the offender. How much should you trust the offender at each level of rebuilding? Depend heavily on the leading of God's Spirit.

8. The evidence of emotional healing is being able to remember the experience of being sinned against without emotional pain at the memory. An offense can be forgiven while the memory is still painful. The pain (without resentment) is an indication that emotional healing is still needed even though real forgiveness has been extended.

Keep in mind that emotional healing is usually a process that happens over a period of time that varies depending on the depth of the need. Major healing events often come along with gradual healing from abiding in the Lord daily. Don't be discouraged when old hurts you thought had healed come to the surface. They will usually be weaker than before—showing that some healing has taken place but simply isn't yet complete. Don't feel condemned—just give those feelings back to God and ask for one more wave of healing by His Holy Spirit.

9. Where possible, do something that shows love for each person you have forgiven (Luke 6:27–28). This loving action, combined with continued prayer, will help bring the right feelings of love and compassion for the offender.

The right decision of your heart makes the forgiveness real—having the right feelings in your heart toward your offender shows that forgiveness is complete. When you can remember the offense without pain, you know the healing is complete. Persist until you are healed.

Plan of Action 9. Forgiveness is perhaps the most neglected and misunderstood area in the average Christian's life. The enemy wants us to believe that Jesus didn't really mean what He said in Matthew 6:14–15 and 18:35. Faithfully point out to the new believer the necessity of forgiving others. Failing to forgive has eternal consequences. (This is the only issue in the Lord's Prayer that Jesus reinforced immediately after giving the prayer to the disciples.) As always, be diligent in your own life in asking for and extending forgiveness. The new believer will pick up on any pretense in your counsel if you yourself have not forgiven those who have wronged you. The new believer must know that this is a serious life-or-death issue. Help him or her to be faithful to God's Word in this critical heart issue.

Reminder: Things to Do This Week

1. Pray each morning that God will give you a spirit of forgiveness. Look forward to the privilege of forgiving someone during the day, and then do it! At

the end of the day, thank God for each opportunity you had to forgive. Ask God to further bless the person you forgave.

2. Continue your daily quiet time study of Matthew 6:1–15, and work through Session 10 before your next meeting on:

 This is a truly important session to understand and to respond to with an honest heart. What God will do in response to your honesty and effort will be life changing!

Freedom through Dependence

A local church's men's group decided they'd mentor younger men who seemed to need guidance in dealing with the challenges of genuine Christian living. One older man who had found the Lord late in life owned an auto repair shop where he employed a rather timid eighteen-year-old who had recently become a believer. The boy's father had been sick most of the young man's life, which left him timid and in need of fatherly influence.

One day at the shop, a customer arrived to reclaim his pickup truck—to be told that the truck was not ready due to problems uncovered that required additional repair work. The customer asked to see the boss and began loudly cursing and swearing about the unexpected delay. The young man watched with interest to see the boss's reaction. The boss chose to respond with the Lord's help:

By depending on God, you are free to live as God intends.

"Pardon me, sir, but every time I hear someone talk like that, it reminds me that I used to talk like that. But Jesus came into my life three years ago and cleaned up my mouth. Now whenever I hear this kind of talk, I have to stop and thank Jesus for what He has done for me. Hold on just a moment."

The boss looked upward and, eyes open, calmly said: "Jesus, You know I used to talk like this gentleman—but when You came into my life, You cleaned up my mouth and gave me a whole new way of talking. Just have to stop and thank You for that." The boss then looked at the customer and said, "Okay, sir, how can I help you?"

In response to the man's tirade, Satan was poised to inspire a sinful reaction and a bad example to the watching young man. However, the boss turned upward and allowed the Lord to determine his response. Righteous witness was given to the customer and helpful example to the young man. "Thy kingdom come" was fulfilled a little more that day.

Discipler Helps

As always, process this session in a fresh and prayerful way in your own heart and life before attempting to guide your new believer. As you discuss the material, your honesty and transparency regarding your own battles, plus the sincere example of your personal warfare, will be of great help and encouragement to the new believer. Assist him or her in following through on the practical steps under the Plan of Action. Don't hesitate to call in extra prayer support and people with greater experience in dealing with satanic strongholds in people's lives.

Part 1

God will provide spiritual protection for you.

 Read Matthew 6:13.

A. When you're tempted, you are enticed to do wrong for pleasure or gain (James 1:14). You want to do or have something that God, in His loving wisdom, does not want for you.

1. You sin when you give in to temptation and offer yourself as a slave to impurity and wickedness to obey its demands (Romans 6:12, 19). James 1:14–15 explains it this way: "Temptation comes from our own desires, which entice us and drag us away. These desires give birth to sinful actions. And when sin is allowed to grow, it gives birth to death" (NLT).

2. Your natural self has many strong desires that are not God's will for you. Things you see, feel, and hear increase these desires. Study Galatians 5:16–21. What are some things that tempt you?

3. You are tempted when you see in your mind pleasurable reward for a sinful action that seems within your reach if you act now to get it. The desire for instant gratification hides the real meaning of the action and the results that will come later (James 1:15). You are deceived if you believe that trading short-term gain for long-term consequences is good for you. (What was Eve thinking when she committed the first sin, as recorded in Genesis 3:6?) Never forget or ignore the truth that sinful pleasure now always brings much grief and pain later.

4. Don't dwell on what tempts you. The longer you think about an immediate reward for sin and hold on to the desire to have it—the stronger your desire will grow and the weaker your will to resist grows. Avoid tempting situations or looking at things that bring sinful pleasures to mind, and you will find it easier not to sin. And whenever sinful pleasures do come to mind, replace them quickly by turning your mind to thoughts you know would please God. Memorize Philippians 4:8. What are two pleasures that strongly attract your natural self when you think about them? What will you do to safeguard yourself against them?

B. You can often avoid temptation. That's the reason for Jesus' words in Matthew 6:13.

1. You can often escape temptation by staying away from situations you know will stir your desire to sin. For example, if God has delivered you from alcohol, what kind of places should you not go, or what kind of situations should you avoid, to help yourself remain free of it?

2. When you cannot escape being in a place where there are tempting influences (for example, someone at your job who is sexually attractive), you can strengthen your heart and mind before you go there. Ask God to help you see that person through His eyes, as a person who is precious to God, rather than as an object for your mental or physical pleasure. Study God's Word (such as Matthew 5:28; Colossians 3:1–3; Romans 6:6, 11) and pray for the Spirit to make it powerful in you. When the tempting situation comes, instead of offering any part of yourself to sin and becoming a slave to its demands by giving in to temptation, exchange that action for the action commanded in Romans 6:13, 16, 19. Summarize what these verses teach you to do when tempted.

3. Ask God for the needed fruit of the Spirit (Galatians 5:22–23) to be at work in you when you need it. Write again the two pleasures that most strongly tempt your natural self. Then, for each one, write the fruit of the Spirit that would be a righteous replacement for that fruit of the flesh.

Temptations:	Fruit of the Spirit:

Temptation seeks to entice you to sacrifice your long-term good for short-term pleasure. Giving in makes you a slave and leads to death (Hebrews 11:24–26).

Part 2

God rescues you from temptation and from spiritual attack.

 Read Matthew 6:13.

A. Evil accurately describes the deception, slavery, and destruction brought by sin and Satan (John 8:44). Following are some major evils. Give some examples of each in the space provided.

1. The bondage of sinful habits (Ephesians 2:1–3; 5:3, 18)

2. The deception of wrong thinking (Ephesians 4:14, 17–19)

3. Satan's harm (2 Timothy 4:16–18)

4. Direct contact with evil powers (Ephesians 2:2; 6:12)

B. Jesus provides freedom from these evils (John 8:31–36; Ephesians 1:19–23).

1. What is your part in this resistance or rescue operation? (See Matthew 6:13; Ephesians 6:10–20; James 4:7.)

2. In the name of Jesus, dismiss from your life every evil spiritual power and activity you were involved with, and destroy any objects that went along with these practices (Deuteronomy 7:25–26). Read 1 John 4:4 and Ephesians 1:19–23, and don't be afraid!

 Romans 6:4–14; 8:31–39 is true. Act on this truth with faith and persistence. God promised victory, so don't stop until you've won.

Plan of Action

 God's plan for you, His child, is to depend on Him for spiritual protection.

1. "Rescue us from the evil one" (Matthew 6:13 NLT) is a battle cry of victory for the believer. Be careful to follow through on the promise in this line of your model prayer, the Lord's Prayer. Break away from Satan's power in your life and the evil activities that are chains of bondage. Some habits and demonic

connections are not easy to break, but if you persist, God will help you be free of them. What is the promise of 1 John 4:1–4?

2. Do not be afraid of the evil one (Satan and his evil spirits), because he is no match for almighty God. Remember the end of the Lord's Prayer: "Thine is the kingdom, and the power, and the glory, forever. Amen" (Matthew 6:13 KJV). Also, remember Ephesians 1:19–22.

3. Steps to freedom:

a. Describe any sinful activities or habits that still have a grip on you.

b. Describe any contacts you still have with spiritual powers, objects, or practices—demonic games, Ouija boards, séances, idols, spiritualistic rituals, charms, fortune-telling, etc.

c. Tell God you are sorry for your involvement in these things. Then act on James 4:6–8. The promises here are:

The commands are:

d. Read Ephesians 6:10–13; Psalm 2:3; Psalm 118:10–14; and Psalm 129:1–4 to strengthen your faith. Pray, guided by James 4:6–8, and resist the devil. In the name of Jesus—by His authority—break the powers of sin and Satan that have held you captive through bad habits, and dismiss the evil spirits that have had a grip on any area of your life. Speak to them directly in the authority of Jesus' name. Also, destroy any occult or magic objects (charms, idols, fortune-telling cards, etc.) you still possess. Whatever spiritual resistance you experience, don't back down! If you stand firm in God's strength, Satan will flee from you. Read 2 Corinthians 10:3–5.

If you or your family are under any kind of covenant with satanic spirits (curse) entered into by you or previously by relatives or ancestors, break that curse by naming it and coming against it in Jesus' name. Use the words of Psalm 118:10–14 as your prayer. Where it says "all the nations" (verse 10), instead put in the name of the spiritual system or kind of spirit you have been linked with (such as witchcraft, masonry, occult group, false religion, etc.). Pray with confidence, "because the one who is in you is greater than the one who is in the world" (1 John 4:4). It is best to have a strong Christian friend or pastor pray along with you for these kinds of tough spiritual battles.

Plan of Action 3. Express to the new believer that obedience to the truths of the last session on forgiveness are essential to releasing God's delivering power. Unforgiveness allows Satan to remain in whatever place of control a believer has allowed him to occupy. Point out how these commands and truths build on what has preceded in the Lord's Prayer and how all these directives for daily living are aspects of God's kingdom coming and His will being done on earth.

4. God is your rescuer and your refuge. He is greater than any evil practice or power you will encounter. Your heavenly Father will deliver you if you call on Him for help, continue to trust His power, and obey any instructions that He gives you in the process. Remember 1 John 4:4 and Ephesians 1:19–22, and live in peace and fellowship with God.

Reminder: Things to Do This Week

1. This unit truly deals with very important issues that affect your life. In coordination with Session 11, study Galatians 5:16–25 in your daily quiet time. Work through Session 11 before your next meeting on:

2. Look for a new way each day to depend on God.

Remembering Jesus Together

When three Ryan brothers were killed within days of each other during World War II, the military moved swiftly to extract from combat the family's sole surviving son, James Ryan. The 1998 blockbuster film Saving Private Ryan *tells the story of a special squad of soldiers assigned to locate James Ryan somewhere on the front lines at Normandy to keep one family from being entirely wiped out in serving their country. Captain John Miller heroically leads the squad on its dangerous mission. He saves Ryan, but at great cost, losing most of his men and being mortally wounded himself.*

As he lays bleeding and dying on a bridge in Normandy, Captain Miller addresses his poignant last words to the man he died to save: "James…earn this. Earn it."

At the movie's conclusion, we see an older James Ryan standing with his family at Captain Miller's grave. Ryan grapples with understanding the captain's enormous sacrifice—giving his own life to save Ryan's—and he contemplates whether his life has honored that great sacrifice. "Every day I think about what you said to me that day on the bridge," Ryan says. "And I've tried to live my life the best I could. I hope that was enough." In remembrance and gratitude, Ryan honors Miller's sacrifice by saluting his grave.

Discipler Helps

When you take part in the Lord's Supper, come ready to remember the price He paid so you could come to the table.

This memorable fictional story helps us understand the enormity of the real story of Jesus' sacrifice to save us. He sought us out behind enemy lines and made it possible for us to get "home" safely. He died so that we might live. All He asks in return is that we remember Him and honor His sacrifice when we partake of communion, or the Lord's Supper. "Do this in remembrance of me," Jesus commanded His followers at that first communion (1 Corinthians 11:24). And again, Jesus said: "Examine yourself before eating the bread and drinking the cup" so as to eat in a manner that is worthy or appropriate to His sacrifice for us (1 Corinthians 11:28 NLT).

If our heart is right toward Him, then we will live our lives submitted to His lordship. We need to examine our lives to assess the level of devotion evident in our attitudes and actions. We can never deserve our Lord's sacrifice for us, but we can love and appreciate Him sincerely and live lives of gratitude to Him for inviting us to His table and paying so dearly so He can have communion with us.

Jesus showed His disciples this special way of remembering after they ate the Jewish Passover dinner together the evening before He died. (The Passover was a special time each year for remembering and celebrating God's rescuing the Jews from slavery in Egypt. You can read the story in Exodus 11 and 12.) He gave His disciples communion to replace Passover because His followers can now celebrate deliverance from sin's slavery and eternal punishment. See Matthew 26:17–29 and 1 Corinthians 11:23–26.

 Read 1 Corinthians 11:23–30.

Part 1

 Communion helps us remember and honor Jesus for giving himself for us and to us.

 Read John 6:47–59.

A. Jesus said the communion bread was like His _____ provided for _____ (1 Corinthians 11:24).

    1. Jesus took the bread and _____ it for the disciples to eat. This was symbolic of the breaking of His body in death to give life to those who would "eat" (John 6:51).

    2. Jesus gave the disciples the broken bread, which they took and ate. Read 1 John 5:11–12, and review John 6:51, 57–58.

        a. A person must "take" or receive _____ to have eternal life (John 1:12).

        b. Eating the bread symbolizes Jesus' coming to live inside us, mixing together His life and our life in a close, ongoing relationship. In fact, the one who eats the bread of communion should be responding to Jesus' presence as he or she is eating! This is the reason for the term *communion*, which speaks of our sharing in the life and presence of Jesus. The bread itself is just bread, but it is important in that it helps us remember Jesus' sacrifice for us.

3. Jesus told His disciples—including you—to "do this to remember me" (1 Corinthians 11:24 NLT) (literally, "be mindful of me") as they ate the broken bread. Jesus had given himself for them then but also now gives himself to His friends by being present with them always. That is why this ceremony is a time of present communion with Jesus around a symbolic dinner table.

B. Jesus said the cup of wine was like the new covenant (relationship) He was offering to mankind, paid for with His blood (1 Corinthians 11:25).

1. The cup of wine is a reminder that Jesus was crushed to release His life-purchasing blood. In what ways would wine be an appropriate symbol of Jesus' blood?

2. Jesus gave His disciples the cup, from which they all drank. Review Matthew 26:27–28 and John 6:53–56.

   a. One must enter into this covenant or new relationship and agree to follow whatever Jesus has planned, just as the disciples drank what Jesus had already put in the cup (1 Corinthians 11:25).

   b. Willingly drinking the cup speaks of willingly entering into a life-giving relationship with Jesus (John 6:54–56).

3. Jesus told His disciples—including you—to remember as they drank the cup that Jesus had poured out His blood for them then—but also being aware that He pours out His love to us now by being present with us always.

C. At the Lord's Supper, Jesus wants us to look with Him to the future (1 Corinthians 11:26).

1. As you share or have communion with Jesus at the Lord's Supper, what should you be thinking about besides Jesus (Matthew 26:29; 1 Corinthians 11:26)?

2. Read John 14:3; 1 Thessalonians 4:13–18; and 1 Corinthians 15:50–53. How and in what condition will we arrive at the place Jesus has prepared for us?

 When we eat the bread and drink the cup in the communion ceremony, we remember and honor the broken body and poured-out blood of Jesus in the past. In the present, we recognize and experience His presence with us as we participate.

Part 2

We ought to examine ourselves before we eat of the bread and drink from the cup in the communion ceremony.

Read 1 Corinthians 11:28.

A. God is not satisfied with religious ceremony if a person is not sincerely worshiping from the heart. Read John 4:20–24.

The Bible says a person may be eating the bread and drinking the cup of the Lord in an unworthy manner (1 Corinthians 11:27). Note: The emphasis here is on the right manner or way in which a person should eat and drink—not on the person's worthiness of this privilege. The word *worthy* in the original language means "fitting" or "appropriate." Why is it wrong for a person to eat and drink in an unworthy manner? (Look again at 1 Corinthians 11:27.)

The right (fitting, appropriate) way of eating and drinking is to do it from the heart—sincerely remembering Jesus' death and responding to His presence now. Your actions should honor Jesus as the source and redeemer of your life. If you are truly honoring Him from your heart, then you are eating and drinking in a worthy manner. Why would it not be right for a nonbeliever to take part in this communion observance?

B. God will discipline a Christian who is eating and drinking for the wrong reasons (1 Corinthians 11:20–22, 27–32).

　　1. Some of the Corinthian believers were coming for the Lord's Supper but not thinking of the Lord (verse 20) or the other members of His body who had come to worship with them (verses 22, 29). From 1 Corinthians 11:21, 34, what does it seem they were thinking of instead?

　　2. How serious was their offense in God's eyes (1 Corinthians 11:27)?

　　3. God's judgment was not to reject them. What did God allow to happen to them and for what reason (1 Corinthians 11:30, 32)?

　　God's discipline should help us correct our behavior, which will then help us avoid the dangers of continuing in sin. Do you examine your own heart and life each day to see if anything in you might displease God?

C. Self-examination is an important part of the Christian life. (Think carefully about 1 Corinthians 11:31; 2 Corinthians 13:5.)

　　1. How can you avoid being disciplined by God (1 Corinthians 11:31)?

 Some translations say we should "judge ourselves," which means to examine ourselves before the Lord to see if our thoughts and actions are right. If we do this by our own choice, God does not have to get our attention through discipline.

　　2. What then should you do before sharing in the communion ceremony (1 Corinthians 11:28, 31)?

　　3. When you examine yourself and discover some sin of thought or action, what should you do before taking part in the Lord's Supper? (See 1 John 1:9.)

　　4. Should you examine yourself only before taking part in the Lord's Supper? Why or why not?

The Lord's Supper is a frequent occasion for you to carefully examine yourself before God. You should act according to 2 Corinthians 6:14–7:1. Then celebrate Jesus' sacrifice for you and His presence with you.

Plan of Action

The spiritual person evaluates everything, including—or especially—the self! Time for a check-up.

Use your quiet time each day this week to work on writing in your answers to the following personal review to help you evaluate your progress in getting to know God through learning to communicate and walk with Him. Discuss your answers with your friend when you and your friend both have plenty of time to talk.

1. Do you have deep and ongoing peace and security with your heavenly Father?

   a. Review your understanding of God's grace.

   • Review Ephesians 2:1–9 and write, in your own words, a definition of what it means to be saved by grace.

   • Do you feel like a beloved child of God as described in Ephesians 5:1; Romans 5:1, 5; 8:14–17? Explain.

   • How have you seen God keep His promises in your life?

   • Have you experienced God's blessing as described in Matthew 5:10–12 while being treated badly for being a Christian? Describe your experience.

Plan of Action. This review will check the new believer's progress and correct failures. It also reviews the benefits of grace—rest in God, resource and room to grow, and certainty for the future. Much is given of a practical nature for you to discuss and reinforce with the new believer. This lesson is intended to help the new believer to:

• Celebrate that God loved him just as he was, but loved him too much to leave him in that condition.

• Give praise to God for the special changes that testify to a real work of grace in her life.

• Be confident of God's acceptance on the basis of parent-child relationship—not on the basis of performance.

• Serve God out of gratitude and as a result of fellowship with Him.

b. Truly good actions are a result of God's grace in your life.

- Summarize in your own words the truth expressed in Ephesians 2:10.

- What good works have resulted from grace in your life?

Contract

Because of God's grace, you can go all out with Jesus (John 15:4–5, 14–15; Romans 8:12–39) without worrying about having to earn salvation. Be confident that God loves you always as His child—that His love is not based on how well you do each day. Your actions of obedience can and should be expressions of gratitude and love, not out of obligation or some misguided attempt to repay God for His goodness toward you. Prayerfully review Romans 8:12–17, 23–39.

Can you say without hesitation: "I have permanently joined myself with God through Jesus Christ and will stay with Him no matter what happens to me"?

Signed _____

Acts 11:23

---

2. How has your life changed since you became a Christian on _____ (date)?

a. Describe internal changes in you. Consider things like feelings of guilt and fear, values (use of time and money), thought life and attitudes, etc.

b. Describe changes in your relationships with people. Consider your ability to forgive; communication levels; and your interaction with family, non-Christian friends, persons in authority over you, enemies, and other Christians.

c. Describe your daily relationship with God.

- What is your view of God now as opposed to how you saw Him before you became a Christian?

- How has your worship changed and grown?

- How often do you remember God's presence and talk with Him? What do you say to God when you think of Him during the day?

- Have you heard God speak to you? About what?

- Do you obey these impressions in your heart or mind? What have been the results of this obedience?

- When do you have your daily quiet time? For how long?

  Benefits:

  Struggles:

 ## Reminder: Things to Do This Week

1. Remember to discuss both sections of this personal review with your Christian friend. Be sure to thank God for what He has done in you and for you in the short time that He has been living in you.

2. Work through Session 12 before your next meeting with your Christian friend on:

Spiritual Living

BILLY
John William Hall
Born Jan 30, 1937—Died July 24, 1937
"He will wipe away every tear from their eyes.
There will be no more death or mourning or crying or pain,
for the old order of things has passed away."
Revelation 21:4

Cuba Hill and John Hall were missionaries whose singular devotion to God and His will took them separately to neighboring West African countries. They grew up on opposite coasts and left by cargo ship from New York City a week apart—John bound for Nigeria, and Cuba for Upper Volta (now Burkina Faso). They met in Africa and returned for furlough as husband and wife—a match made in heaven.

Soon they were blessed with a spunky little girl, Evelyn, and they returned to Upper Volta, where they pioneered the work in Ouahigouya, 110 miles north of the capital city of Ouagadougou. Soon little Billy arrived—healthy and full of smiles and life.

Cooperating with and depending on the Spirit means your day-to-day life will be holy.

When he was just four months old, Billy developed blackwater fever and dysentery, complicated by malaria. For two months, while fellow missionaries and African saints fervently prayed, the parents tenderly cared for their struggling baby with round-the-clock vigils, meager medical intervention, and fervent prayer of their own. At 3 a.m. on July 24, Billy's spirit left his little body and heartbroken parents—and was welcomed into heaven.

John and Cuba stood by the small casket and renewed their consecration to the Lord, asking Him to give them, in the place of their little darling, many souls born into the Kingdom. Cuba wrote to her parents: "Through it all, the Lord has been so good and has upheld us and sustained us. He means more to us than ever before, and there is a fresh longing in our hearts for His coming. Since our trust is in God and we are serving Him, we haven't really lost our Billy—we shall have him again. The Lord is seeing us through."

John and Cuba Hall are a testimony of behavior that displays the fruit of the Holy Spirit within them. Obvious fruit included their continued love for God in spite of unanswered prayer for healing and for the Africans they came so far to serve. They demonstrated the fruit of peace that sustained them as they grieved the death of their child. The fruit of faithfulness kept them on site reaching Africans—whom they would continue to serve over a span of fifty-one years. They retired at age seventy-five and are now in heaven with Jesus and Billy. Their four surviving offspring rise up to call them blessed and give thanks for their heritage.

Part 1

Stay in touch and in step with the Spirit.

 Read Galatians 5:16, 25.

A. Speak often with Him, with all kinds of prayers (Ephesians 6:18).

B. Listen continually to hear the Spirit speak to you (John 15:4).

C. Believe that God will help you do what He says to do (Philippians 4:13).

D. Believe that God will do what He tells you to pray for (John 14:13).

E. Memorize God's promise and plan for you in Romans 8:28–29. Read on to the end of the chapter.

F. Be with other Christians often, at regular meetings and in between, to allow the Spirit to work in you through others, and through you to others. Carefully read Matthew 18:19–20 and Hebrews 10:23–25.

We are to live and walk by the Spirit. This means we must not go our own way and expect Him to come along behind. Rather, we should keep in step with Him as He leads us.

Part 2

The Holy Spirit lives in and acts through you to make you like Jesus.

A. Be like Jesus (Romans 8:29). Follow carefully the directions and examples from the Bible.

1. Jesus lived the top two commandments: love God and love people (Matthew 22:38–40).

2. The way Jesus lived is described in John 13:1–17; 21:1–14. Jesus lived in complete cooperation with the Holy Spirit, as described in Galatians 5:13–14, 22–23.

3. Now consider the Holy Spirit's role in Jesus' life as described in Luke 4:18–19 and Acts 10:38. What or who was flowing out of Jesus?

4. Read Galatians 5:22–23 to learn how you can live like Jesus with the Holy Spirit flowing out of you.

B. Cooperate with the Spirit. When you cooperate with Him, the Holy Spirit reproduces in your life Jesus' loving attitudes and actions. This is the fruit of the Spirit (Galatians 5:22–23)—what the Spirit produces in your life.

1. According to Romans 5:5, from where does this fruit come?

2. Make a list from Galatians 5:22–23. "The fruit of the Spirit is…"

3. Which fruits have you seen most often in your life?

4. Which ones seem weakest or don't appear often?

5. In John 21:15–19 Jesus explained to Peter how to obey the top two commands to function as a pastor. In what ways did Peter need the fruit of the Spirit to accomplish what Jesus was saying he should do?

2.A.4. Picture yourself as a bucket, with water flowing out of you. For that to be happening, what else has to be happening? Water has to be flowing into you. And so it is with the Spirit and God's love. If the Holy Spirit's love is to flow out of you to others via the fruit of the Spirit, you must also be receiving an inflow of the same (Romans 5:5). God never asks us to give something He has not first provided. So the issue is not whether we have the goods to live holy lives. When we have the Holy Spirit, we have all we need already inside. The issue is releasing the Spirit and His resources that are already in us.

2.B. Your honesty and openness about your own struggles, victories, and failures in this personal battle of every Christian to live godly lives in Christ Jesus can be of great help and encouragement to the new believer who is needing to lay hold of a functional spiritual lifestyle. Emphasize to him or her that perfection is not attainable in this life but only when we are glorified after death. However, we can and must progress and grow. New believers feel encouraged when they pass a spiritual marker from time to time and realize that they're not what they used to be, but they're also not yet all they're going to be. Encourage the new believer to read Galatians 5:22–23 as a picture in faith of what he or she will be like in the future, as the Spirit is given more and more room to operate. That should be an exciting perspective, as opposed to the depression inspired by reading that passage and considering how hard it is to function that way in one's own strength.

C. Recognize when your behavior is not from cooperating with the Spirit.

    1. List the behaviors described in Galatians 5:15, 19–21, 26 that were part of your life before you came to Jesus. List also the fruit of the Spirit.

Fruit of my natural self:	Fruit of the Spirit:

    2. Circle those behaviors you still find yourself doing. Place a check beside the one that is hardest for you to not do.

    3. Ask God to help you exchange these sinful behaviors for behavior (fruit) the Spirit will produce. Which kinds of spiritual fruit are needed to replace each kind of natural fruit that you listed under the fruit of your natural self? Draw lines to connect the natural fruit with its spiritual fruit replacement.

"The heart is more deceitful than all else and is desperately sick; who can understand it" (Jeremiah 17:9 NASB). The human heart by itself can produce nothing but sin even when sincerely trying to do good (Romans 7:14–23). Only the Holy Spirit within you can produce fruit and behavior that is holy.

Part 3

Release the Holy Spirit to be holy and loving through you.

 Read John 15:1–12.

A. You decide the winner of the battles inside of you (Galatians 5:16–17).

    1. Identify the two opponents squaring off against each other in Galatians 5:17.

    2. You pick the winner of each battle by giving in to the desire of your _____ or by turning to the _____ to help you act His way.

B. Pray every day to win the battle for that day (John 15:7).

    1. Pray every morning, guided by Galatians 5:16, 22–25. Write down the guidelines for praying that you see in this passage.

    2. Pray specifically every morning for God to help you:

        a. Turn away from the desire to do what you listed under the fruit of your natural self (2.C.1.).

        b. Turn to the Holy Spirit to produce holiness through the fruit of the Spirit in your behavior, especially the fruit you listed as missing under 2.C.3.

    3. As you go through the day, silently ask God to help you respond with the fruit of His Spirit to each person and situation you encounter.

C. Depend on the Holy Spirit to win each battle (John 15:4–5; Romans 6:11–19).

    1. Turn away from sinful desires (Romans 6:11–13).

        a. Verse 11: Consider yourself to be _____ to sin, which makes it possible for you to do as described in verse 13.

        b. Verse 13: What does this verse give as the action that is the alternative to being dead to sin?

        Example: A natural thing to do when someone hurts you is to give yourself to anger, allowing it to direct and fuel your reaction. Play dead to such feelings and turn away from them and their influence so that you can…

    2. Turn to the Spirit.

        a. First, remember that you are considering yourself to be _____ to God and _____ to sin (Romans 6:11–12).

        b. Then, follow verse 13 and present yourself to God to receive instruction as to what to do next instead of doing what your natural self is urging you to do. All the members of your body are alive from the dead (ready for action), and are ready to be instruments or tools of _____ as directed by God (Romans 6:13).

        Note: The pattern of this action is familiar. You've had a lot of practice with allowing strong feelings—such as anger—to guide and provide

3.C.2.b. The gripping idea in these passages in Romans 6 is that the pattern for holy behavior has been learned in the flesh—in our natural way of life—as we have often "presented ourselves as slaves" (i.e. yielded) to the sinful desires of the flesh, allowing those desires to inspire and direct our behavior. A life of faith is not some unobtainable mystery but a well-rehearsed pattern now centered on the Holy Spirit instead of the flesh. Now, with the Spirit's constant presence, we can always turn to Him, yielding ourselves to His inspiration and direction for our behavior. The crux of the matter is not being ignorant of how to let the Spirit work in us but rather our willingness and desire to do so moment by moment, every day. Satan tries to block us from being dependent on the Spirit, working overtime to blind us to how much we do know already.

energy for your actions. Now just change the direction you turn. Turn to the Holy Spirit and give in to His influence. He will help you respond with the fruit—the character—of the Spirit as Jesus did. Write in your own words the instructions in Romans 6:19.

Example: When you are angry, you should turn away from the temptation to react in anger and instead present yourself to God to release the Spirit-fruit or fruits of _____ to operate instead of anger.

The fruit of the Spirit needed for a holy response is available to you when you turn to the Holy Spirit in any situation. The more you allow the Spirit's responses to replace your natural reactions, the more you will have and demonstrate to other people the character and love of the Spirit. To help your heart beat along with God's heart, follow the Plan of Action below.

Plan of Action

God's plan for you, His child, is to live a life of holiness.

1. Stay alert to the Holy Spirit. This is essential for releasing the fruit of the Spirit (John 15:4–5). As you continue your walk by the Spirit (Galatians 5:16, 25), make every activity of business, study, conversation, planning, or pleasure a joint project or shared experience with God. *I* has now become *we*. Life has no more private experiences. Sharing them all with God gives them much greater value to you and to God. God has promised to guide you and provide for you in whatever way you need, but your mind and heart must stay attentive to God.

   Remember, John 10:4 and Romans 8:14 are both promises and commands. As you stay tuned in, you will hear His voice. And the more you obey the voice of God in your heart and through His Word, the sharper your spiritual hearing will become, the more His power will flow through you to help you obey, and the sweeter will be your fellowship with God.

2. Ask God to help you have His heart for people, demonstrated by:

   a. Eyes that see needs. According to Matthew 9:36, what need did Jesus see?

b. Real concern for people with needs. In Matthew 9:36, how do you know Jesus was concerned for the people?

Psalm 126:5–6: "He that sows in _____ shall reap with _____."

Rewrite John 11:33–35 in your own words.

In Acts 20:31, what did Paul have plenty of as he cared for people?

c. Willingness to enter their needy, painful world...

- In prayer. Read Matthew 9:38. Rewrite Galatians 4:19 and Colossians 4:12–13 in your own words.

- In service. Rewrite 2 Corinthians 3:3 and 1 Thessalonians 2:7–12 in your own words.

Reminder: Things to Do This Week

1. Resume your daily quiet time, studying Galatians 5:19–25 and completing your Daily Journal.

2. Complete Session 13 before your next meeting on:

Going with the Flow

Painful as it was to lose their infant son, John and Cuba Hall— missionaries to Burkina Faso, West Africa—determined that they would not quit doing what God had called them to do. They trusted in the Lord and leaned on Him in their sorrow.

They noticed that the Africans were watching them closely, and after a while, many of them began asking questions. Infant mortality is so high in West Africa that nearly everyone has lost one or more children. For them, death is devastating because they have no hope for the future. When someone dies, family and friends wail and scream and beat their chests in despair because they believe the evil spirits have come and stolen their loved one's soul away.

When people saw that the Halls did not mourn like that, they wanted to know why. It gave them many opportunities to tell about Jesus, His sacrifice for them, and that His death and resurrection conquered death and gives assurance of eternal life. Only eternity will show how many souls were won for the kingdom of God as a result of Billy's death.

John and Cuba found new meaning in 2 Corinthians 1:3–4, where the apostle Paul wrote: "Praise be to the God and Father of our Lord Jesus Christ, the Father of compassion and the God of all comfort, who comforts us in all our troubles, so that we can comfort those in any trouble with the comfort we ourselves have received from God." The Halls praise God for the comfort they received that allowed them to give comfort to others.

Pray for more workers, and for great effectiveness in their work.

Billy's death appeared to be a calamity and brought great sorrow to his grieving parents. However, God's divine purpose was accomplished through his early departure. The Spirit worked through the Halls, powerfully increasing their witness to the saving truth of Jesus Christ. This is an example of moving in the flow of the Spirit—working *with* the Spirit in Jesus' name, not merely working *for* Jesus. Witness to Jesus requires supernatural power

Discipler Helps

This is an important lesson for the new believer. And it can bring anxiety for you when it comes to praying with him or her to be filled with the Spirit. Completing this session and its instructions can give God a chance to do an important work in both the discipler and the new believer.

The goal of the session is to help the new believer understand the promise of and the purpose for the infilling of the Spirit—and then to receive this infilling for the same reason God provides it, and having the results that God intends. Encourage the new believer to live in the fullness of the Holy Spirit, constantly surrendering to Him and demonstrating Spirit-controlled behavior.

along with human effort to follow the instruction of the Spirit and God's written Word (Acts 1:8). Pray for workers who will flow with power—and keep in the flow yourself. The potential harvest is great, and workers full of the Spirit's power are the key (Matthew 9:38).

 Read Acts 1:8.

Part 1

 **God gives ability from above for workers to be effective in doing His work on earth.**

 Read John 1:32–34; 16:7–15.

A. Jesus himself relied on this ability from above to be effective in ministering to others.

   1. Luke 4:18—"The _____ of the Lord is _____ me, because he has anointed me."

   2. Acts 10:38—"God anointed Jesus of Nazareth with the _____ and _____, and…he went around doing good and healing…because God was with him."

B. Just before returning to heaven, Jesus talked to His disciples about this help from above.

   1. What did Jesus tell them to wait for (Acts 1:4–5)?

   2. Who would baptize them in the Holy Spirit (John 1:33–34)?

   3. In Acts 1:6–9, Jesus told His followers:

      a. What would happen. (Describe it here.)

      b. What they would become. (Summarize it here.)

c. Where they would do this. (Define their mission field here.)

4. According to Luke 24:49–53 and Acts 1:13–14, what did the disciples do in Jerusalem?

C. After the Holy Spirit was poured out on them, the disciples became Christ's witnesses. Read the exciting story in Acts 2 through 4. (Note: Being filled with the Spirit is the same as being baptized in the Spirit. When a person is baptized in the Holy Spirit, he or she receives ability from God to say and do things he or she could never do alone—which shows that God's power is working through that person.)

1. New abilities. Read Acts 2:4, 6, 11, 14–18, 36–41. What did the Holy Spirit do through people and in people on the Day of Pentecost?

2. New power. Read Jesus' promise in Mark 1:16–18: "I will make you _____ of men." How does Acts 4:31 show this happening?

3. Changed lives. Peter experienced a big change in his life.

a. Describe Peter before he was filled with the Spirit (John 13:36–38; 18:1–27).

b. Describe Peter after he was filled with the Spirit (Acts 4:13; 5:17–32). What can you tell about Peter's change of character by what he wrote in 1 Peter 3:8–17?

4. Continuing mission. Read about other Christians in the early church who were filled with the Spirit (Acts 4:31; 8:14–17; 9:17; 10:44–47; 13:52; 19:1–6). Notice the things they did as they were controlled by (filled with) the Spirit.

a. According to Acts 2:39, who does God want to have this experience of being filled with the Spirit?

b. Does this mean you, too? Do you want to be filled with the Spirit? Explain.

Summary. It would be helpful at this point to give personal testimony to the new believer of your own experience of being filled with the Spirit and the change it brought to your life—both in your prayer life and in the extra power and ability gives you. Describe different experiences people have had when they were filled, and the similar effects. Point out that speaking in tongues is usually the immediate result of being filled with the Spirit that you can observe but that Jesus said the reason for the Holy Spirit coming upon believers was to assist them in witnessing for their risen Lord. Emphasize that becoming equipped to accomplish God's work should be the reason the new believer desires and seeks to be filled with the Spirit. Other blessings are real and important but should be seen as secondary to and supportive of the primary reason. Point out that the Spirit gives us abilities to accomplish whatever God tells us to do but that the ongoing experience of speaking in tongues should make it easy to have faith that the same Spirit will readily speak through us in the new believer's own language with the right words to speak in the opportunities arranged by the Spirit. The key to Spirit-given ability to witness is our constant dependence on the Spirit.

2.A.3. It may be important to help the new believer identify and surrender every area where he or she is consciously holding back. Don't put a heavier burden on the new believer than what the Spirit is putting on him or her by pointing out all the shortcomings you see. If the new believer seeks to be filled with the Spirit and seems to encounter a roadblock, pray and ask God to help you point out possible reasons for the delay. Encourage the new believer to inquire of the Lord and receive firsthand conviction rather than going on secondhand conviction (yours) in seeking to be filled. If the Spirit doesn't convict him or her of what you

 You are baptized in the Holy Spirit the first time you surrender to the Spirit so deeply that He gives you words of praise to God in a language you don't know—and you actually say them out loud. This gives you faith to surrender again and again, receiving ability from God to say and do things you could never do alone (Acts 1:8). This allows people to see Jesus at work through you. As Jesus' witness, you will do and say the things Jesus did and said. And you will tell who Jesus is and how He arranged for us to be with Him forever.

Part 2

You can receive this ability from above.

A. Prepare to receive.

1. Jesus wants you to receive power so that you can be what? (Read Acts 1:8.) Do you want more power—the ability—to tell other people about Jesus?

2. Read John 7:37–38. Jesus invites you to come to Him and drink if you are spiritually thirsty for more. How thirsty are you? Explain.

3. Jesus wants your complete surrender, and you want rivers of living water to spring up inside of you, giving you power to be His witness. Ask Jesus to show you anything you are holding on to in your life that hinders you from being baptized in the Holy Spirit and what you should do about it. Then do it. Write what needs to change and how the Holy Spirit directs you to make the needed change. Copy what you write to a prayer list for daily reference.

B. Pray in faith that you will receive (Luke 11:9–13).

1. Ask Jesus to baptize you in His Holy Spirit (John 1:33). Your part is to surrender completely so the Spirit can take control.

2. Now begin to praise Jesus with joy (Luke 24:52–53) because He has saved you and is going to baptize you in His Spirit. You know He will, because He promised He would in Acts 2:38–39. So go ahead and thank Him!

3. As you praise Him, concentrate completely on Jesus the baptizer. He will make you know (give you faith) that if you will begin to speak, the Spirit will give you His words. (Acts 2:4 says the believers gathered were all filled with the Holy Spirit and began to speak in other languages as the Spirit enabled them.) When the faith comes to you that you can speak with words supplied by the Spirit, begin to speak—but don't use your own words. Just say the words the Spirit gives you. Because it's a new experience, you may feel awkward—but just relax and let the new praises flow. Praying this way will soon feel natural.

4. If there is a delay in your being filled, don't be discouraged. God is delighted in your coming. Go back to point A.3, surrender yourself to Him, and keep seeking.

5. This experience is a beginning…so continue it daily—and powerfully!

Being filled with the Spirit and speaking a new language is impossible to do on our own. Jesus is the one who baptizes you in the Holy Spirit. Prepare to receive, pray to receive, and then power up.

Plan of Action

God's plan for you, His child, is to become a worker in His harvest with the Holy Spirit's help.

1. You can pray to be baptized in the Spirit when you are alone—but don't hesitate to ask others to pray with you. Keep in mind that God delights in every sincere move you make toward Him, so don't be discouraged by delays. He has promised to baptize you in His Spirit—"The promise is for you and your children and for all who are far off—for all whom the Lord our God will call" (Acts 2:39). That includes you, so go on seeking until you are filled—not with worry but with genuine thirst for God and confidence in the outcome.

2. Keep in mind that being baptized in the Spirit is not the end or even the highest point of your spiritual journey. God intends it to be the beginning of a Spirit-powered life in which you witness about Jesus' love and see the lost transformed by that love. You should be praying in a Spirit-given language frequently, and you should be stepping out daily in the flow of the Spirit to help people around you put their faith in Christ.

have pointed out, don't press the issue—unless, of course, it is a clear violation of Scripture and the godly alternative is clear.

2.B.3. The key to taking much of the stress out of seeking to be baptized in the Spirit is the instruction given here: "When the faith comes, you begin to speak." Encourage the seeking new believer to focus on Jesus, not primarily on speaking in tongues. Speaking in tongues is an act of faith—God and man working together. So until the new believer has faith to speak in an unknown language, point him or her toward Jesus, the baptizer, until He gives the necessary faith. Encourage the new believer to act on the faith that he or she has received. Take care that the manner in which you assist the new believer in seeking to be filled with the Spirit does not distract him or her from focusing on Jesus in praise and with expectation.

Some people must be left alone before they can overcome their self-consciousness and concentrate on the Lord enough to receive their baptism. Pressing a person to continue until he or she receives may merely increase frustration. However, if the new believer wants to persist in seeking and praying, continue with the new believer as a supportive friend.

2.B.4–5. Reinforce point 4 (about seeking) as long as appropriate, and then reinforce/encourage point 5, about practicing the new prayer language daily. At times you may be told that someone has been filled with the Spirit but has not spoken in tongues. Don't have a doctrinal argument over the impossibility of that happening. Instead, point out that the usual pattern in the New Testament is that being filled with the Spirit is followed by speaking in tongues. Then say something like: "So, in order to make your experience fully biblical, go ahead and speak in tongues, because being filled with the Spirit gives you the ability to do so. Remember the apostle Paul's statement: "I wish that you all spoke in tongues" (1 Corinthians 14:5 NASB) and "Pray in the Spirit on all occasions with all kinds of prayers and requests" (Ephesians 6:18).

3. Memorize the F-L-O-W outline below that explains Acts 1:8. Use it as a prayer guide and plan for witnessing and harvesting.

   a. Faith in God (God-confidence that overcomes fear—Acts 4:29–30)

- Alert to the Spirit leading you to nonbelievers
- Trusting the Spirit to work through you and in them

   b. Love from God

- His love coming to me for others through His Spirit within (Romans 5:5)
- His love being released through me to others (fruit of the Spirit: Galatians 5:22–23)

   c. Openings by God

- Looking for doors opened by the Spirit for witnessing (Colossians 4:2–6)
- Opening my mouth with boldness from the Spirit (Ephesians 6:19–20)

   d. Winning the nonbeliever to faith in Christ (2 Corinthians 3:2–6) by the Spirit's drawing (John 12:32)

- Gaining the nonbeliever's trust as a friend through kindness and listening
- Persisting until the nonbeliever's trust is placed in Jesus (Matthew 16:16–17)

Note: Peter's confession was by revelation, not by human observation—in spite of how close Peter was to Jesus.

 Without the Spirit, we cannot succeed in the harvest—but in the F-L-O-W of the Spirit, we cannot fail.

 ## Reminder: Things to Do This Week

In your quiet time study each day, make notes on the F-L-O-W in Acts 1 through 12.

Sowing Gospel Seed

A friend brought a recently released felon to a pastor to hear the good news of Jesus. The pastor told the man that Jesus had died on the cross for his sins, and he urged him to ask forgiveness for those sins. That news sounded good to the felon, but he struggled to understand how it could work for him. Then a thought occurred to him: "Pastor, do you mean that Jesus took the rap for me?" The pastor agreed that was exactly what Jesus had done. He was then able to lead the man to a faith commitment to Jesus, who truly had taken the rap for him on the cross.

Missionaries arrive on foreign soil realizing that they must translate the good news into the local languages for people to understand and be saved. The same principle is essential within subcultures and differing life experiences even when people speak the same official language. The apostle Paul realized this and adapted his vocabulary and approach to fit the mind-set of his listeners. (See 1 Corinthians 9:19–23 and Acts 17:16–33.) Paul even asked the Colossians to pray that he would be able to make the good news clear to his various listeners, and he encouraged the Colossians to know how to respond to each person when they witness (Colossians 4:3–6). This principle applies in modern Western society as well. When we translate the unfamiliar truth into familiar terms, people who hear us can understand, and Satan is not allowed to steal it away.

We should know the truth that each hearer needs to understand—and also prepare ourselves to explain it clearly in the vocabulary of the individuals who stand before us. This will enable them to know the truth and be saved.

This session contains the essential truth of the gospel with clarity regarding what lost people need to know to be found.

Discipler Helps

These last two sessions provide a condensed course geared to equip the new believer to be a witness. The new believer must intensely wish to move from the "childhood" era of his or her Christian life to the grown-up stage—becoming a spiritual parent to nonbelievers and spiritual babies. Don't rush the lessons, but emphasize their importance and the need for the new believer to work hard to memorize the essential information needed for faithful personal evangelism.

Your role as discipler can be extremely helpful in setting up opportunities for joint witnessing, such as street witnessing events or talking together with non-Christian friends or relatives of the new believer. Nothing is better than firsthand observation by the new believer and on-the-job training as he or she participates in increasing measures in the joint witnessing events. The discipler's role should gradually move from main operator to partner to observer—all the while providing evaluation of what is taking place. Invite input from the new believer on how you did in the witnessing he or she watched—both positive and negative. Such discussion will benefit both of you and will reinforce the valuable attitude of openness to constructive criticism out of a sincere desire to grow and improve in serving our Lord.

The true nature of harvest activity should be firmly fixed in the new believer's mind. The sensitivity and attitude of the laborer toward God and toward lost people will be determined largely by how he or she sees the nature of the task at hand.

Part 1

God loves you and wants you to be close to Him as His child— now and forever.

 Read John 1:12, Romans 8:15–17.

God's whole plan for your life with Him—as His child—is described in the following three activities you should continue to do:

A. Receive God's love through faith in Jesus Christ (John 3:16).

   1. Put your faith in Jesus, and then believe that His Spirit has come to live *in* you and is giving you God's life and love (Romans 5:5; 8:9–11).

   2. Receive through Jesus the provision of your needs—forgiveness, guidance, the ability to obey God, and material supply—by His Spirit (Matthew 6:33; John 15:4–5).

B. Respond to God with sincere love and worship (Luke 10:27).

   1. Repent of sin and be thankful for His love (Acts 2:38; 1 John 4:19).

   2. Depend on His Spirit in everything you do and for everything that you need (John 15:4–5, 14).

C. Release God's love through you to other people (Luke 10:27).

   1. Forgive and love others from your heart as you are forgiven and loved by God (Luke 10:27, 33; 11:4).

   2. Show love to people in actions and words by cooperating with the Holy Spirit (Luke 10:34–37; Galatians 5:22–23).

God's whole plan for your life with Him as His child is in the three activities described above. To help you remember, write in the missing words to complete the following outline:

1. _____ God's love through _____.

2. _____ to God with _____.

3. _____ God's love through _____.

Part 2

You can become God's beloved child and have this wonderful life trusting Jesus as your sacrifice (sin payment), your Savior (helping friend), and your Lord (leader).

 Read Romans 10:12–13.

 Read John 3:16; 1:12; 15:14 and then follow these steps:

A. Ask Jesus to forgive you, and accept Him as your sacrifice, your sin payment (John 3:16).

   1. Believe that Jesus' suffering and death was full payment of the penalty for your sins, so you don't have to pay for them forever in hell (Matthew 20:28; John 1:29).

   2. Trust Jesus to forgive you of your sins so you won't go to hell for being a sinner and so your life now will not be controlled by sin (John 3:16; Romans 8:1–4).

B. Believe in Jesus as your living Savior and your helping friend forever (John 1:12; 15:14).

   1. Believe that Jesus rose from death to life and is now able to give you eternal life as God's child (John 1:12; Romans 6:21–23).

   2. Trust Jesus to put His Spirit in you and to help you with everything you need for your life (John 8:31–36; Romans 8:8–11, 35–39).

C. Cooperate each day with Jesus as your leader and Lord (John 15:14; Romans 6:22).

   1. Believe in Jesus' purpose and plan for your life on earth (Luke 9:24; Romans 8:28).

   2. Trust Jesus as your leader by cooperating with Him in everything you do (Luke 9:23; Romans 8:13–14).

2. Help the new believer get the outline of the gospel—ABC: Sacrifice, Savior, Lord—firmly in mind, along with the accompanying Bible passages (John 3:16; 1:12; Luke 9:23; John 15:14). Many times the opportunity for witness does not allow for opening a Bible and having the nonbeliever read various passages. However, the written Word of God is powerful and anointed and should be read directly whenever possible. The new believer should be prepared to turn to appropriate Scripture passages when the opportunity arises.

Keep in mind, however, that the Spirit will always anoint the truth—whether it's read, quoted, or paraphrased. The early Christians had no pocket New Testaments—not even a Bible in their homes—and no tracts. What they did have remains as the most important human tool for proclaiming the gospel—their voices. They used theirs—and we must use ours. (See Acts 8:4.)

When you receive Jesus, you are born of the Spirit (John 3:5). You become a member of God's family and begin a whole new life—forgiven and able to experience God's provision and the blessings of cooperation with God—for eternity.

To help you remember how a person becomes God's child through Jesus Christ, write in the missing words:

A_____ _____ from Jesus, your s_____ (sin payment).

B_____ in Jesus as your living S_____ (helping friend).

C_____ each day with Jesus as your L_____ (leader).

Now memorize this simple outline (Sacrifice, Savior, Lord) and the three main Bible verses (John 3:16; 1:12; 15:14). It will be a great help to you in sharing the gospel with lost people.

This material will prepare you to clearly share the good news as you follow the leading of the Spirit in reaching out to lost people.

Remember that a clear explanation needs to be accompanied by a clear example of Christian character. The fruit of the Spirit should be evident in your life.

According to the Bible, the primary reason for salvation is to bring people into fellowship with God—not just to rescue them from hell. A new believer needs to combine faith and effort each day in his or her spiritual childhood to learn how to live in continual fellowship with God as outlined in Part 1. Keep in view that the goal of evangelism is to bring people into an ongoing relationship with God through Jesus Christ, not just a brief encounter with God. Study the next session carefully to learn how to help a nonbeliever begin and continue to live in fellowship with God.

Write in the missing words from John 14:6. Jesus said, "I am the _____, the _____, and the _____. No one _____ to the Father [God], except _____ me." Do you understand what Jesus said well enough to be able to explain it to someone else?

Plan of Action

God's plan for you, His child, is to reach out with the good news about Him to lost people.

1. Pray with your Christian friend for specific people you are witnessing to—that God will help you lead them to Him.

2. Carefully choose a few nice-looking tracts that also have a clear message similar to what you have learned in this unit. Give them to people you meet. Be sure to give them with love and a smile.

3. A person who wants to become a Christian often needs help putting his or her commitment to God into words in prayer. Write out and memorize a faith commitment prayer so you will be ready when God gives you opportunity to lead someone to Him. Your preparation will be a step of faith that God will, in fact, give you this opportunity to help someone give his or her life to God. Use the "ABC—Sacrifice, Savior, Lord" outline as a guideline for writing a faith commitment prayer that is faithful to the gospel message. After you have written it, review it and see if you have included all the basic elements that a person needs to know to decide to make a serious, lasting commitment to Christ. Here is a sample prayer:

Jesus, I believe that You are the Son of God and that You died to pay for my sins against You. I am sorry for my sins, and I ask You to forgive me.

Jesus, I believe that You rose from the dead, and I ask You to come live in me and be my friend forever. I believe You will provide eternal life as God's child and whatever I need each day.

Jesus, I believe that You have the best purpose and plan for my life. I want to cooperate with You as my leader and depend on Your help for everything I do. Thank You for loving me so much that You have made my heart Your home. I love You, Jesus. Amen.

You might also share with this new spiritual baby in the family that he or she needs continuous contact with God to have continual conduct with God.

4. In Session 15 you will learn how to use the information you learned in this session. These last two sessions are extremely important for you to learn well and remember long. Other people's eternal lives depend on your being well equipped to lead them to Christ. So please put forth extra effort to study thoroughly these long sessions—for the sake of the lost people around you. Keep in mind that you are studying for their sake, not just for yourself. And use Ephesians 6:19–20 as a guide for your praying.

 ## Reminder: Things to Do This Week

Work through Session 15 for the study part of your daily quiet time. Session 15 is especially long and important to understand, remember, and practice continually. Be thorough in discussing this unit with your Christian friend when you meet on:

Reaping

In his teen years, Dawson Trotman spent his energies gambling and pursuing other youthful pleasures in his home city of Los Angeles. At age eighteen he began courting Lila, a pretty girl whose first love was Jesus. She wouldn't associate with Dawson unless he attended her church. At his first church meeting, Dawson was assigned six Bible verses to memorize. At the second meeting, Dawson was the only one who had memorized them all. The same thing happened at the third meeting. While trying to impress Lila, the truth he was taking in took him in, and he began a personal relationship with the author of the words he'd memorized.

His experience convinced Daws that memorizing the Bible was the key to having a strong Christian faith. He also became passionate about personally introducing others to the Jesus he had met in the Scriptures. He began to organize youth groups and hand out scores of Scriptures to be memorized. One day in 1934, a mother asked him to visit her son, a sailor.

The sailor and Daws sat in his old car near the dock, and Trotman quoted the Bible to the young man until a policeman became suspicious. Trotman talked the officer into joining them for prayer. The young sailor said: "I'd give my right arm if I could do what you just did." That sailor led a friend to Christ with the approach he learned from Trotman, and that new believer in turn convinced another. Dawson's movement, eventually known as Navigators, spread across the seven seas—at one point during the war having a presence on more than a thousand ships and stations. With the help of converted sailors reentering society along with a partnership with the Billy Graham crusades, Navigators grew and eventually included multitudes on land worldwide.

This session will help prepare you to be sent into your world to advance God's kingdom by increasing its citizens and the level of their service to the King.

Discipler Helps

Spiritual birth occurs in several ways. The apostle Paul reported to the Galatians his spiritual struggle on their behalf: "My dear children, for whom I am again in the pains of childbirth until Christ is formed in you" (Galatians 4:19). Along with the agonized push of intercessory prayer, there is a need to understand what is happening in the person hearing your witness— where they are in their spiritual journey—so you can focus on helping them take the next step. If you do the right things at the wrong times, the process is hindered—much as in a natural childbirth event. Laboring with God requires alertness to what our role is at any given time, based on where the lost person is in his or her journey. The witness should also continually be aware of the main role that God always plays in the process.

Upon learning of Trotman's death, Billy Graham spoke for many Christians in many places of the world: "I think Daws has personally touched more lives than anybody I have ever known.... He lived to save others."

Along with many Navigators, you have benefitted from being mentored in your new faith in Jesus. This experience has prepared you to be a mentor to serious inquirers and to other new believers. As Jesus commanded, pray that the Lord of the harvest will send workers into His harvest (Matthew 9:35–38). Then volunteer to be part of the answer to your prayer. Will you say to the Lord of the harvest, "Here am I, Lord, send me"?

 Read John 4:35–36.

Part 1

Teamwork between believers and the Lord of the harvest is the process for reaping.

Following are the visible and invisible phases through which a nonbeliever passes on his or her way to new B-I-R-T-H. The Holy Spirit and the cooperating laborer work together in each phase. It is helpful to find where a lost person is to know what the next phase is on his or her journey.

A. **B**ridge—a Spirit-arranged contact that inspires interest and trust in the non-believer toward the laborer, allowing further contact for witness (John 4:7; Acts 8:26–31; Acts 10:19–20)

    1. The laborer makes contact as prompted or arranged by the Spirit.

    2. The Spirit begins by preparing the nonbeliever's heart and then arranges contact with the laborer.

B. **I**nsight—a sinner's God-given recognition of sin, separation from God, and the need for forgiveness (John 16:8)

    1. The laborer helps the nonbeliever recognize and admit his or her need. The laborer identifies the needs by observation, inquiry, or revelation from the Spirit.

    2. The Spirit convinces the nonbeliever of his or her need.

C. Revelation—when the nonbeliever knows in his or her spirit that the gospel is true (Matthew 16:17)

   1. The laborer explains the content of the good news, clarifying that Jesus must have authority over our daily lives (Romans 10:14).

   2. The Spirit convinces the nonbeliever that the good news is, in fact, true.

D. Trust—when the nonbeliever repents of sin and puts his or her faith in Jesus Christ (Romans 10:9–13)

   1. The Spirit influences the nonbeliever to choose to give in to God's love (Acts 16:14). Unless prompted otherwise by the Holy Spirit, generally the witness should see evidence that the Spirit is drawing a person before encouraging the nonbeliever to trust Jesus.

   2. When it is evident that the Spirit is drawing the nonbeliever toward a faith commitment, in a gentle, nonpressuring way, the laborer invites and encourages the nonbeliever to pray to put his or her trust in Jesus as their leader and friend. If the nonbeliever agrees to do so, the terms of the contract should be reviewed and the nonbeliever encouraged to pray his or her own commitment prayer. If the person wants your help in praying, help as explained below. Avoid pressuring the nonbeliever into a premature birth (Matthew 13:20–21). If you do assist people in praying a commitment prayer:

      a. Explain that it is their prayer if they mean it from their heart.

      b. Keep the words simple and common so they can understand immediately and easily make what you say their own prayer. (It is helpful to have a commitment prayer in everyday language already prepared.)

      c. Make the prayer easy to follow by leading slowly and using brief phrases.

      d. Lead in a prayer that is not too short (omitting essentials) or too long (tiring or confusing to the person).

E. Home—the new believer is born of the Spirit when the Holy Spirit comes to live in the new believer, who now belongs to God as His child. God is now Father, and other Christians are brothers and sisters.

   1. The laborer accepts the newborn as a brother or sister and rejoices in God's grace.

   2. The Spirit of adoption enters the new believer and becomes the spiritual connection with God and other spiritual family members.

1.D.2. The witness needs to recognize first when the Spirit is pulling, and then give a gentle push—being careful to avoid human pressure. The nonbeliever must respond to the Spirit for true conversion to take place—not just go through the motions to avoid being rude to the witness who is exerting pressure.

Help those who clearly want to make the commitment to trust but hesitate by sharing some personal testimony of overcoming hesitations to accept Christ. Often there are no real obstacles in the nonbeliever's way—just a natural or Satan-inspired hesitation to put it off. Overcome this by asking the question: "Can you think of any good reason to not receive Jesus into your life right now?" Often the answer will be: "Well, not really. You mean right here?" And your answer: "Yes! God is right here waiting for you to put your trust in Him." Then proceed to the salvation prayer, even if you are in a public place. Do not require the nonbeliever to close his or her eyes. God will hear just the same, and the person can concentrate more on praying than on wondering whether someone is watching.

3. Older family members disciple the new member in how to live as a member of the family of God.

 God activates each B-I-R-T-H stage during the conversion process. Be observant and alert through the Spirit to recognize each stage and cooperatively follow His lead as you labor with Him (John 5:19).

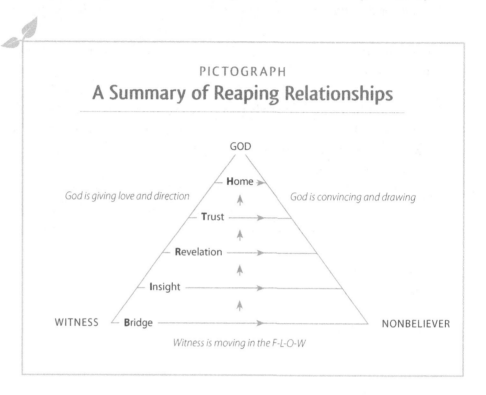

PICTOGRAPH

A Summary of Reaping Relationships

GOD

God is giving love and direction   Home   *God is convincing and drawing*

Trust

Revelation

Insight

WITNESS   Bridge   NONBELIEVER

Witness is moving in the F-L-O-W

Pictograph. Review with the believer the stages in witness, showing how God works on all sides of the triangle. Use the comments listed below to assist you in explaining the triangle of relationships, progressing as in building a house—from the bottom up.

Teamwork between God and Man (John 5:19):

1. God begins the work in a nonbeliever's heart.

2. God arranges contact between the nonbeliever and a believer and activates His love in the heart of the believer for the nonbeliever.

3. God instructs and empowers the believer for witness.

4. God anoints the spoken witness as the believer gives it.

5. God waters the seed in the nonbeliever's heart, giving divine revelation of the love of God in Jesus Christ.

6. God pulls the nonbeliever toward himself as the believer gently pushes.

7. God and the believer accept and welcome the new child home.

Part 2

The Lord of the harvest seeks discipling friends to help Him preserve the harvest by helping new believers learn to live their new life.

A. The new believer needs a friend to L-O-V-E him or her with God's love (1 Thessalonians 2:7–8). Here's how:

1. **L**ike the new believer—show warmth.

2. **O**pen your life to the new believer for a two-way friendship.

3. **V**alue the new believer as a brother or sister and as a precious child of God.

4. Encourage the new believer to stay faithful in contact and conduct with God (Acts 11:23).

B. The new believer needs a discipler to H-E-L-P him or her learn to walk with God (1 Thessalonians 2:9–12; 4:1–2).

1. **H**ear—really listen to—the new believer to understand him or her.

2. **E**xplain the truth in terms the new believer can understand, in response to questions and needs, using the sessions in *THRIVE*.

3. **L**ead the new believer by example, practical instruction, encouragement, and accountability.

4. **P**ray for the new believer daily and diligently.

 A Discipling Friend who L-O-V-Es a new believer will H-E-L-P him or her learn to walk with God. A church family that loves its new members will joyfully receive them, value them, and help them become a functioning part of the body of believers.

Part 3

The Lord of the harvest seeks more workers.

Read Matthew 9:37–38.

A. Only people who have been harvested can be workers (Acts 4:20). They can:

1. Share the message with full conviction that it is true (1 Thessalonians 1:5).

2. Explain the message from personal experience (1 Thessalonians 1:5; 2:10).

B. Workers are people who pray (Matthew 9:38; Ephesians 6:19). They pray:

1. That the Lord of the harvest will send out workers (Matthew 9:38).

2. For themselves as they obey His command to go (Mark 16:15; Acts 1:8).

   a. For words that are _____ (Colossians 4:3–4, 6).

   b. For conduct that is _____ (Colossians 4:5).

3.B.2.a. Discuss with the new believer the need to speak clearly and graciously without needing to be eloquent. The Holy Spirit will help us speak with grace and will help the non-believer understand and accept, but we have a responsibility to prepare ourselves as best we can in advance to be used by the Spirit. That is why it is so important to work hard on Sessions 14 and 15 and pray hard for love (grace) for lost people.

c. For a manner that is _____ (Ephesians 6:19–20).

3. For an _____ door for witness (Colossians 4:3).

4. For God's help in _____ the opportunity (Colossians 4:5).

C. Workers cooperate with God as they labor. Review how Jesus cooperated with the Father by reading John 5:17–20; 8:28; 4:35–38.

1. Cooperative workers are alert to what the Spirit is doing in a nonbeliever (John 5:19).

a. They know the steps the Spirit takes to draw a person to himself—as outlined under B-I-R-T-H.

b. They are observant of circumstances (like the good Samaritan—Luke 10:33).

c. They are good listeners who seek knowledge through conversation (as with Philip and the Ethiopian—Acts 8:30–37).

d. They are sensitive to revelation from the Spirit (see John 4:17–18; Acts 8:26; 16:9–10, 18).

2. Cooperative workers act in partnership (cooperation) with the Spirit.

a. They respond to obvious needs according to the principles of God's Word unless directed otherwise by the Spirit (as did the good Samaritan—Luke 10:34–35).

b. They are led by the Spirit in ways that are unexpected in the natural view of things (as with Philip and the Ethiopian—Acts 8:26, 29; and Peter and Cornelius' household—Acts 10:19–20).

Plan of Action

God is sending you, His child, to work with Him to gather the harvest.

1. Have you been sent by the Lord of the harvest?

a. To whom?

b. To do what?

c. Does your heart beat with God's heart—full of love for lost people? Are you constantly praying for God to give you His love?

2. How would you evaluate your obedience in witnessing and discipling new Christians?

a. Strongest areas:

b. Weakest areas:

3. Find a Bible passage to guide your praying for each of the weak areas listed above. Make a prayer list, writing each need area followed by the Bible passage that speaks to that need. Leave space beside each item to write in answers to prayer as they come.

Prayer List Sample

Need: Lack of love for the lost

Prayer: Matthew 9:36 (NASB): "Seeing the people, He felt compassion for them." Lord, help me to see people's needs and feel Your love for them.

Answer: (Write how God is giving you His love for people you know, and give their names.)

Prepare for a lifetime of winning people to Jesus.

1. Prayerfully review the F-L-O-W progression in Session 13, giving close attention to the two points under each letter. Write the outline on a sheet of paper, and put it in your Bible or prayer notebook to use as a frequent guide for praying. Plan regular times to pray through this outline on a daily or weekly basis.

Prepare. Take plenty of time for thorough and practical assistance as the new believer struggles through these assignments. Eternity is at stake for some people in connection with our ability to communicate well. Do some role-playing with the new believer to help him or her get these small but strategic blocks of conversation into well-functioning order.

3. B-I-R-T-H stages Illustrated:

Jesus and the Samaritan (John 4:3–43; Jesus models the role of the human partner with God)

1. Bridge: God arranged the contact, and Jesus built a bridge for meaningful communication with the Samaritan woman.

2. Insight: Jesus helped the woman have insight into her own sin and need for a savior.

3. Revelation: The Holy Spirit revealed to the woman that Jesus is, in fact, Savior and Lord.

4. Trust: Based on her belief in who Jesus is, the woman put her trust in Jesus as Savior and Lord.

5. Home: This lost woman could now address God as her Father—she had come home. She instinctively began to help with family business by building a bridge between the townspeople and Jesus (witnessing).

Philip and the Ethiopian Official (Acts 8:26–39)

1. Bridge: An angel told Philip to take the road to Gaza where he saw the official riding and reading. "The Spirit told Philip, 'Go to that chariot and stay near it.' Then Philip ran up to the chariot and heard the man reading Isaiah the prophet. 'Do you understand what you are reading?' Philip asked. 'How can I,' he said, 'unless someone explains it to me?' So he invited Philip to come up and sit with him." What a great example of a Spirit-given bridge.

2. Insight: The official asked for guidance and explanation of what he was reading. He was quite open about his need to know more about God.

3. Revelation: "Then Philip began with that very passage of Scripture and told him the good news about Jesus" (Acts 8:35). (This extended conversation became a discipling

---

2. Memorize the B-I-R-T-H outline and the two points under each letter, a job-description for the Holy Spirit and you. Rehearse it with a friend to help fix it in your memory. If you keep in mind what you and the Spirit are to do in each phase, you can cooperate more closely with the Spirit.

3. Make your own outlines of the B-I-R-T-H stages in the stories of Jesus' winning the Samaritan woman (John 4), Philip winning the Ethiopian official (Acts 8), and Peter winning Cornelius and his household (Acts 10).

4. Memorize the "ABC—Sacrifice, Savior, Lord" outline of the gospel from Session 14, along with the points under each main point. Without referring to any written source, write a sinner's prayer that includes the elements of the outline above. Compare it with the one you wrote in Session 14, and revise it until you are satisfied. Now commit it to memory in faith that you will be using it—soon!

5. Write out an up-to-date testimony to help you explain Christian living in practical terms.

   a. Focus primarily on your current relationship with Jesus. (You don't need a dramatic conversion experience or a bad past life to have a testimony worth sharing. If you do have those things, don't talk much about them. Instead, talk mostly about your present relationship with Jesus.)

   b. Use words that are understandable to an unchurched person, just as Jesus used everyday language and illustrations.

   c. Write a two-minute version and a five-minute version so you can be prepared for opportunities of varying time lengths.

6. Witness to a nonbelieving friend by reviewing your assignments with him or her. Be alert for the Holy Spirit's arranging other opportunities (bridges), and be conscious of His presence to help you while you are sharing. Also be alert to His working in the heart of your friends before, during, and after your sharing. In other words, tune into the F-L-O-W of the Spirit so you can do your part in bringing God's love to people. You can certainly depend on the Spirit to do His part.

7. By doing the *THRIVE* sessions with the help of a discipling friend, you have been preparing yourself to be a discipling friend to someone else in need. Winning someone to Christ and helping that new brother or sister establish his or her own contact and conduct with God is the most important reason for being alive.

experience that preceded the faith commitment by the official and continued to the point of water baptism after his commitment.)

4. Trust: The official announced his faith in Jesus and asked to be baptized.

5. Home: Philip baptized him, and the official "went on his way rejoicing" (Acts 8:39).

For further illustration of the Home level activity, consider the implications in the homecoming of the prodigal son (Luke 15:11–31).

The father welcomed his lost son home with open arms and great rejoicing. Having received forgiveness, the returned son could now live under the supervision of his father, carrying out his assigned responsibilities in coordination with his older brother. It was the father's desire for his older son to help welcome his lost-and-found brother and to work alongside him and guide him to help carry on the family business. The older brother's responsibility was to disciple the younger brother.

❧ CONGRATULATIONS ❧

You have completed the **THRIVE** sessions with the help of God and your discipling friend. But your real spiritual foundations are not complete until you are actively involved in winning others to Christ and being a discipling friend to them—just as someone has been to you. Never stop eagerly responding to God's loving presence by loving Him in return and by loving others in teamwork with Him. Be the best discipling friend to young believers that God can help you to be!

May the Lord of the harvest send you daily into His harvest. "Go and make disciples… And surely [He is] with you always, to the very end of the age" (Matthew 28:19–20).

Appendix A | Daily Journal

DATE _____ PASSAGE _____ VERSES THAT SPOKE TO ME _____

WONDERFUL THINGS I SEE _____

_____

_____

_____

HOW THEY APPLY TO MY LIFE _____

_____

_____

_____

PRAYER NEEDS _____

_____

_____

_____

PRAYER VICTORIES _____

_____

_____

_____

Appendix B   How to Be a Discipling Friend

Introduction

A literal translation of Jesus' words in Matthew 28:19 is, "Disciple all the nations." God intends for His spiritual family to love His newborn spiritual children and work with Him to disciple them until they are strong and able to disciple others. You have been discipled by someone using these **THRIVE** sessions. Now you can be a discipling friend to another new Christian using a new copy of these same sessions.

Part 1

God intends for His older children to receive new Christians as their own brothers and sisters (Luke 15:32). This includes:

A. Celebrating with God the birth of new members of His eternal family (Acts 11:23).

B. Receiving new believers in His name as members of the family whom God loves as much as the older family members (1 Thessalonians 2:7–11; 3:12).

C. Being a friend who…

- understands their past,
- accepts them as they are,
- sees the good in them, and
- gently encourages them to grow.

Part 2

God's loving family helps His new children learn to walk with Him (Acts 14:21–23).

A. Paul and his coworkers in Thessalonica…

1. Prayed for the new Christians (1 Thessalonians 1:2–3; 3:9–13; 5:23).

2. Helped them learn to walk with God (1 Thessalonians 2:7 to 3:13; 4:1–8).

3. Helped them learn to love people (1 Thessalonians 4:6–12, 18; 5:11–15).

B. Then the new believers willingly cooperated with their disciplers until they also became disciplers of new Christians (1 Thessalonians 1:6–10; 2:13–14; 4:1, 9–10).

Read 1 Thessalonians 1 through 5 to see the example set by discipling friends Paul, Silas, and Timothy as they cared for the Thessalonian church—and how the Thessalonian believers followed their example, in turn discipling others.

Part 3

Spiritual growth is best served by a discipling friendship between a more experienced spiritual brother or sister and a new Christian.

A. A discipling friend (discipler) is a guide for the new believer.

1. The discipler should explain that the sessions instruct the new believer to learn to walk with God.

2. The discipler helps the new believer to personally experience God's presence and power while learning direct conversation with God through:

   a. Studying His written Word and responding in prayer.

   b. Hearing God speak while praying and through the day.

3. The discipler should pray daily and diligently for the new believer's needs and growth.

4. The discipler will receive from God the help he or she gives to others.

B. A discipling friend should encourage two-way communication by:

1. Being honest and open in conversation.

2. Being a patient and attentive listener.

3. Describing his or her own background and growing experiences to…

   a. Help the new believer understand the growing process in Christian living.

   b. Encourage the new believer to trust Jesus always.

4. Arranging time to be with the new believer without a planned discussion, to allow friendship to grow. In this setting the new believer can talk about things that are on his or her mind and heart or ask questions. This will allow the discipler to better understand how well the new believer is grow-

ing spiritually or where he or she is struggling. "Out of the overflow of the heart the mouth speaks" (Matthew 12:34).

5. Being alert to what God wants to teach him or her through the new believer, because God always works through fellowship between believers to benefit everyone involved.

Plan of Action | The Discipling Process

A. Disciplers need to be trained before they disciple new believers.

1. Disciplers should always work through each session themselves before discussing the material with a new believer. This will help the discipler to know the material well and to be able to help the new believer better understand God's truth.

2. If possible, disciplers should discuss each session with another Christian or in a small group before discussing it with a new believer. This will help them explain things more clearly.

3. Disciplers should bring their completed sessions to the meeting with the new believer as notes for reference.

B. Disciplers need to know how to use the *THRIVE* sessions.

1. First meeting: Go through Session 1 with the new believer, assisting him or her to understand how to work through the material and to understand the truth and how it applies to everyday living. At the end of each meeting:

   a. Explain and assign the daily time of study and prayer (quiet time) to be practiced until the next meeting between discipler and new believer.

   b. Always take time to pray together without hurry, encouraging the new believer to talk to God as simply and naturally as if talking to another person. When you pray, use simple words so the new believer can learn how easy it is to pray by listening to you.

   c. Arrange a regular weekly time to meet. Be faithful in meeting with new believers—even if they are not. Their spiritual life depends on it.

2. Second meeting: Go through Session 2 with the new believer, using the same activity format as with your first meeting. Give whatever help is

needed to find answers in God's Word, and discuss how those answers guide daily living. Review changes in the new believer's life, discuss their quiet-time experiences, and take turns praying. Turn to Session 3 in their handbook, and ask them to work through it on their own before your next meeting. Encourage new believers to give their best effort in completing the material but not to not worry about any difficult parts. Assure them that when you meet, you will discuss and make clear the Bible's answers to the questions.

3. Third meeting: Discuss together the new believer's answers, questions, and other responses to Session 3. At the end of the meeting, give the new believer Session 4 to complete before the next meeting. Continue this process for the remaining sessions.

C. Disciplers should follow these guidelines for discipling others:

1. The sessions usually work best when used by one discipler with one new believer. If many new believers need to be discipled, two or three can meet together with one discipler.

2. Contact the new believer at least once a week without a detailed plan for the conversation. This contact, by phone or in person, will let you check on how well the new believer is doing and will help your friendship grow.

3. Maintain a schedule for completing the sessions.

   a. Meeting regularly is more important than completing an entire session at every meeting. Sometimes dealing with pressing needs in the new believer's life will require multiple meetings to finish a session.

   b. If the new believer seems to be making a real effort to learn and grow, it is important to give him or her whatever time is necessary to understand and apply the truth to his or her life.

Being a discipling friend actually begins with being a friend of sinners, as Jesus is. God wants us to rescue people from the fires of hell, but He also wants us to train (disciple) them to walk with Him in daily fellowship and obedience. An important part of their obeying God is for them to become discipling friends to others. Jesus said, "Therefore go and make disciples of all nations...teaching them to obey everything I have commanded you" (Matthew 28:19–20). So be sure to teach the new believer to disciple others while you also keep discipling new Christians.

Appendix C | Answers

Session 1

1.B.1.a. According to John 3:36, what will happen to every person who does not believe in Jesus Christ?
They will experience the wrath of God.

1.B.1.b. What will such an unbeliever not see or receive?
Eternal life.

1.B.3. When Jesus died, He was being punished for your crimes against God. Why do you think He allowed himself to be treated this way? (For a big hint, see John 6:38–40 and John 15:13.)
Jesus allowed it because He loves me and because it was God's will.

1.C.1. To all those who receive Jesus and believe on His name, what special right does Jesus give them?
Jesus gives them the right to become children of God.

1.C.3. You can now say, "God has put His own Spirit inside of **me** to stay forever."

2.A.1. Because of your spiritual birth, where will you one day be able to go that you would not otherwise be allowed to enter (John 3:3, 5)?
Because of your spiritual birth, you can enter the kingdom of God.

2.A.2. Spiritual birth brings spiritual life. Your new life makes it possible for you to obey your new King, something that was impossible before no matter how hard you tried to be good. Read John 8:34–36. Whose slave were you before Jesus set you free?
Sin's slave. Everyone who sins is a slave to sin.

Session 2

1.A. God loves you greatly, and His Spirit in you brings His love. Find the book of Romans in your Bible and read chapter 5, verse 5 (Romans 5:5). What does this verse say that indicates God is generous with His love?
God has poured out His love into our hearts.

1.B.1. Read John 1:29. God sent Jesus to remove the **sin** from between you and God.

1.B.2. Read John 6:44. Since you have come to Jesus, how does this show that God wanted contact with you before you wanted contact with Him?
God was pulling/tugging me toward Him before I wanted to know Him.

1.B.3.a. What do you have to do so that food and drink can give life to your body?
I must take it into my body.

1.B.3.b. What did you do so that Jesus can give life to your spirit?
I took Him into my spirit.

1.B.3.c. The result, in Jesus' words, is:
I remain in Him, and He remains in me.

1.B.3.d. Read John 14:17. You and Jesus can be "in" each other by His **Spirit** being in you.

1.B.4. God knows everything about you in every area of your life no matter how small it may seem. How does Jesus explain it in Luke 12:6–7?
Although sparrows are many and worth little, God notices each one of them and cares for them. We are worth more than many sparrows, so God is always paying attention to each one of us. God is concerned with every aspect of our lives—so much so that He keeps count of the hairs on our heads.

1.C.1. From Romans 8:16, what is God saying to you?
"You are My child."

1.C.2. From Romans 8:15, what does God want you to say back to Him?
"Father!"

2.A.1. Read Luke 6:12–13. What did Jesus do immediately before He made the important decision of calling His disciples? What role do you think contact with God played in this decision? What lesson can you learn for your own life from Jesus' example?
Jesus spent the entire night praying. No doubt God gave Jesus wisdom and direction for such an important decision. We need to spend time seeking God's will and His direction for our daily lives and all our important decisions.

2.A.2. Read John 4:31–34. What was even more satisfying to Jesus than having a meal when He was physically hungry? This would mean that Jesus; greatest appetite was to do what?
Doing His Father's will gave Jesus more satisfaction than eating when He was hungry. Jesus' greatest hunger was to completely obey His Father's will.

2.A.3. Read John 5:17–20, 30. How did Jesus know what He should do?
The Father showed Him and told Him.

2.A.4. Read John 5:17; 14:10. How was Jesus able to do what He did?
The Father was within Him working with Him and through Him. Jesus did not speak on His own authority, but on behalf of the Father at work through Him.

2.B.1. What is one of God's commands you feel you especially need God's help to obey?
Personal answers will vary. Be sure to pray with new believers about particular areas where they are finding it more difficult to obey God.

2.B.2. Read again John 15:4–5. How successful will we be trying to live for God if we try to do it by ourselves? Does God ever want you to try to accomplish something alone or with only other people's help?
Without God's help and remaining in Him, we will fail and accomplish nothing. God never wants us to go it alone or with only the help of others. We must rely on His help.

2.B.3.a. John 2:1–11:
**Man's part: asked for help, obeyed instructions, and used what was on hand.
God's part: gave instructions, changed water to wine.**

2.B.3.b. John 6:5–13:
Man's part: offered what was on hand and obeyed instructions. God's part: gave instructions and increased the food.

2.B.4. Like you, God enjoys doing things with someone He loves. That someone in this lesson is you. How do you feel about doing things with God?
Personal answers will vary.

Session 3

1.A.1. According to 1 John 4:19, who started loving first, God or mankind?
"We love because he [God] first loved us" (1 John 4:19).

1.A.2. According to Romans 5:6–8, did God love you because you were good?
No.

1.B.1. Read Romans 5:5. How and where does God pour out His love for you?
God's love is poured out into our hearts through the Holy Spirit.

1.B.2.b. Read Romans 8:15–18. You know by the Spirit telling your spirit that you are God's **child**.

1.C.1. Read John 1:12–13. What sort of people have been given the right to become children of God?
All those who received Him, who believed on His name.

1.C.2. Read John 6:55–57. You are allowing Jesus to love you by receiving Him into your life, just as you allow food and drink to help you when you eat and drink.

1.C.2. Read John 6:55–57. You are allowing Jesus to love you by receiving Him into your life, just as you allow food and drink to help you when you **eat** and **drink**.

1.C.3. What has God done for you that helps you understand Him better?
Personal answers will vary.

2.A.1. Can a person receive benefits from God without being grateful to God for what He has done? (See Luke 17:17–18; Matthew 18:27–32.)
Yes.

2.A.2. Why do you think the nine lepers and the forgiven slave were ungrateful? What was different about the one leper who returned?
Perhaps they were too busy enjoying the benefit they had received or were too self-centered. The leper who returned wanted to say thank you and give credit where credit was due.

2.A.3. Which are you more like, the grateful one or the ungrateful nine?
Personal answers will vary.

2.B.1. One leper responded with true gratitude to God. How does the leper's response in Luke 17:15–16 demonstrate true worship?
The returning leper praised and gave glory to God and thanked Jesus.

2.B.2. Read Philippians 4:6 and Ephesians 5:20. What does God desire from you in response to His love for you?

He wants me to continually thank Him.

4.A. With whom does a selfish heart cooperate in sinning (Ephesians 2:2–3)?
Satan

4.A.1. Read John 5:44; 8:23, 34, 38–47; 12:43; and 1 John 2:15–17. These verses show why most people do the things they do. What are some of the reasons?
To get praise or glory from people; because they are of this world instead of from above: because they are slaves to sin; because they are children of Satan; because they love what the world has to offer.

4.A.2. Read Matthew 6:1–8. Why does a selfish heart pretend to worship God?
To be seen by people; to be honored by people; to impress God with "many words."

4.A.3. Does God receive it?
No.

4.B.2. Read John 8:28–29. Even Jesus, the perfect Son of God, did nothing on His own but spoke just what the Father taught Him. What does this passage tell you, Jesus' disciple, about how your actions can be like His?
I should do nothing on my own but only what God tells me to do (through the Bible and His Spirit)—always depending on God and always trying to please Him.

4.B.3. How do worshiping God, talking with God, and obeying God go together? (See John 8:29; 15:14–15.)
Obeying God is: fellowship with God; an act of friendship with God; experiencing God's pleasure; honoring God as supreme in my life.

Session 4

1.A.1. Read John 10:11–18; 27–30 where Jesus calls himself the Good Shepherd. Describe what the Good Shepherd does to show His love for us, His sheep.
The Good Shepherd knows each sheep personally, calls them all by name, talks to each sheep, leads them out, goes before them, protects, provides, guides, is loyal, lays down His life for the sheep, is self-sacrificing, inviting, and gives eternal life.

1.A.2. After Peter had betrayed his love for Jesus and denied Him three times, Jesus gave Peter a second chance to know His love and show it to others. Read John 21:15–17. What did Jesus tell Peter to do?
Jesus told Peter to feed and care for His sheep, thus showing them the same love Jesus had for Peter and all of His "sheep."

1.A.3. Read 1 John 4:21. What do you hear Jesus saying to you? How is it similar to what He told Peter?
Anyone who loves God must show it by loving his or her spiritual brothers and sisters. This is another way of doing what Jesus described as caring for His sheep.

1.A.4. Read the top two commands Jesus identified in Matthew 22:36–39. Write the first, or greatest, command in your own words.
Look for any paraphrase of Matthew 22:37: "Love the Lord your God with all your heart and with all your soul and with all your mind."

1.A.5. Write the second command in your own words.
Look for any paraphrase of Matthew 22:39: "Love your neighbor as yourself."

1.A.6. How can you know what true love is? How can you love as God does? (See John 13:34; 1 John 3:16; 5:2.)
We know what true love is and how to love by observing Jesus' example of self-sacrifice and service. God commands us to love others as He has loved us, to love our brothers and sisters, to lay down our lives for others, and to love God and obey His commands.

1.B.1. All love begins and flows from God (1 John 4:9–10, 16, 19). You must obey the first command by loving God to keep on receiving God's love. According to John 14:20–23, what is the second component besides love?
The second necessary component is obedience, or keeping Jesus' commands.

1.B.2. You can give to others from the love you have received from God, which is obeying the second command. Copy the phrases in 1 John 4:7–12 that tell about loving others out of the love you receive from God
Love comes from God; since God so loved us, we also ought to love one another; if we love one another, God lives in us.

1.B.3. When you love your other spiritual family members this way, what does it prove? John 13:35; 1 John 4:7:
Such love proves that I am a disciple of Jesus, that I am born of God, and that I love God.

1.B.4. How important is it for God's love to be flowing through you to others? (1 John 3:10, 14–15; Matthew 5:43–48)
This is very important. Such love provides evidence of my salvation and shows that I am like my Father in heaven.

1.B.5. How can you know the right way to love your neighbor, as described in the second command (Matthew 22:39)?
I must love my neighbor as I love myself.

1.B.6. The best way of loving yourself is to allow God to love you as you trust and obey Him. The best way of loving your neighbors as yourself is to help them receive God's _____
love

2.A.1. List all the acts of loving mercy that are shown in the story.
The Samaritan—the one who acted like a good neighbor—doctored the injured man's wounds; put the man on his donkey while he walked; cared for the injured man at the inn; enlisted someone else to help; paid for expenses; promised to come back to check the man's progress and pay whatever additional was needed for the man's good care.

2.A.2. Review the story of the unforgiving servant in Matthew 18:27-33. What sort of mercy was needed in Matthew 18:27 and 33?
Extending forgiveness.

2.A.3. Jesus came because His Father loved the world so much (John 3:16). Love cares about needs. What was the greatest need Jesus came to meet? (See John 11:25–26, 40–45; 12:44–50.)
People's greatest need is for eternal life and knowing how to receive it.

2.B.1. When you tell your family and friends about how Jesus has changed your life, you are being a witness about Jesus to them.

2.B.1.b. Tell your story peacefully, with faith that the Holy Spirit will do His part, which is to convict unbelievers of sin, righteousness, and judgment (John 16:7–8).

2.B.2. What does 1 Peter 3:15 tell you to always be ready to do?
I must always be prepared to give the reason for the hope that is in me, and to do it with gentleness and respect.

Session 5

1.A.1. In Matthew 28:19, who does Jesus say to baptize?
Jesus instructed His disciples—then and now—to baptize those they would disciple.

1.A.2. In Mark 16:16 Jesus says: "He who has **believed** and has been baptized" (NASB).

1.A.3. Who was baptized in the early church (Acts 2:38; 8:12)?
Those who repented and believed were baptized.

1.B.1. In Matthew 28:18–20, Jesus gives instructions regarding baptism. These instructions are (circle one) suggestions/**commands**.

1.B.2. When you obey Jesus, you are showing your **love** for Him (John 14:15).

2.A.1.a. God sees you as if **Jesus'** death was your own, because Jesus' death pays in full the debt for your sins (Romans 6:5).

2.A.1.b. Because the penalty demanded by God's law has been paid by Jesus, you are no longer **under the law**, but under grace (Romans 6:14).

2.A.2.a. Romans 6:6–7 says: "Our old self was crucified with him, so that the body ruled by sin might be done away with [or be rendered powerless—the actual meaning of the original language], that we should no longer be **slaves** to sin—because anyone who has died has been **set free** from sin."

2.A.2.b. Romans 6:12 says: "Do not let sin **reign** in your mortal body." When sin reigns, you **obey** its evil desires.

2.B. New Life: According to Romans 6:4, you are raised with Jesus to **live a new life**. That means going under water as if buried—then being raised up as if resurrected with new life.

2.B.1. You are free from sin and free to **live** with Jesus (Romans 6:8).

2.B.3.a. What will happen to your body when it is raised from death (1 Corinthians 15:3–8, 35–57)?
I will receive a new, eternal body–just like Jesus' body.

2.B.3.b. Where will you live for eternity (John 12:25–26; 14:1–3)?
I will live forever with Jesus.

Session 6

1.A.1.   God wants you to see Him and relate to Him **as He is** / as you think He ought to be. (Underline one.)

1.A.2.   God sees you and relates to you **as you are** / as you want Him to see you. (Underline one.)

1.B.2.   Read Romans 8:14–18. Why would God want you to call Him **Father**?
He loves me as His child.

1.B.3.   How is God's father's heart shown in Matthew 10:29–31?
He gives continual and close attention to me as a loving Father does His children.

1.B.4.   The prayer Jesus taught in Matthew 6:9–13 shows you that God, your Father, already wants to do things for you, His child. What are those things?
God wants to give me daily bread, forgiveness, guidance out of temptation, rescue from the evil one.

1.B.5.   According to Matthew 7:7–11, what is one thing you must do to receive from God?)
I must ask and keep on asking.

1.B.6.   What plans does God have for your future (Ephesians 2:6–7)?
He wants to show me His kindness forever.

2.A.   What words here tell of God's authority?
Father, in heaven, your kingdom, your will be done on earth as it is in heaven, deliver us

2.B.   How much authority does God have, and why does He have so much? Think carefully about the passage above as well as about 1 Timothy 6:13–16 before writing your answer.
God has all authority; no one is beyond His reach and no one has equal power. He is the Creator, the source of life; He is eternal and unapproachable.

3.B.   Study Revelation 4:1–11, and write the key words and phrases that describe the holiness of God in heaven.
Sits on a heavenly throne; surrounded by glory; continually worshiped, and described as holy and worthy.

Session 7

1.A.1.   Jesus said that if you **love** Him, you would do what He says (John 14:15).

1.A.2.   Obedience is also an act of **faith** as stated in Romans 1:5.

2.A.   What are God's reasons for having earthly rulers (Romans 13:4)?
God instituted earthly rulers for good of those ruled and the restraint and punishment of wrongdoers.

2.A.1.a. **Governments should commend those who do right and punish wrongdoers—with the sword if need be.**

2.A.1.b. **Job supervisors/employers should do what is right and fair for those under their authority.**

2.A.1.c. **Church leaders should keep watch over the church members.**

2.A.1.d. **Parents should not exasperate their children but bring them up with godly training and instruction.**

2.A.1.e. **Husbands should love their wives sacrificially, be devoted to their spiritual well-being, and love their wives as themselves.**

2.A.2. **God** holds earthly rulers accountable for how they act toward the people under their authority (Romans 13:6; Ephesians 6:9; Hebrews 13:17).

2.B.1. Children are to **obey** their parents (Ephesians 6:1-2). Everyone is to honor his or her parents.

2.B.2. Wives are to **submit** to and **respect** their husbands (Ephesians 5:22-24, 33).

2.B.3. According to 1 Thessalonians 5:12–13 and Hebrews 13:7, 17–19, how should church members treat church leaders?
Church members should respect, love, imitate, obey, and pray for their leaders.

2.B.4. How should employees act toward their bosses (Ephesians 6:5–7)?
Employees should obey their supervisors, respect them sincerely, and serve them from the heart wholeheartedly as if serving Christ.

2.B.5. How should citizens treat civil authorities (Romans 13:1–7; 1 Timothy 2:1–2)?
Citizens must submit to the authorities, do what is right, and pay taxes.

2.C.1. Write the promises of Ephesians 6:1–8.
If we obey and honor our parents, it will go well with us and we will enjoy long life on the earth; God will reward us for whatever good we do.

2.C.3. In Romans 8:28, to whom does God make the promise of all things working for good? Are you included in this group?
God works for the good of those who love Him and who have been called according to His purpose. Personal answers will vary but should be yes.

2.C.7. According to Acts 4:18–20, what should you do when human authorities demand direct disobedience to God?
You should respectfully decline obeying man when it conflicts with obeying God.

Session 8

1.A.1. According to Psalm 24:1, how much does God own? Whose property are you and your things (Psalm 24:1; 1 Corinthians 6:20)?
God owns the earth and all everyone and everything in it. I and all my possessions belong to God.

1.A.2. Read Psalm 104. Is God able to provide for you out of what He has?
Yes.

1.A.3. Read Matthew 6:25–30 and circle the phrase that makes this sentence true: God's resource is sometimes not enough / just enough / **always more than enough to meet my need**. (Think of the implication of the father's statement in Jesus' story in Luke 15:31.)

1.B.1.a. When does He know what you need (Matthew 6:8)?
God knows what I need even before I ask.

1.B.1.b. Think again about what Jesus says in Matthew 6:8, 26, 32. How much do you think He knows about what you need? (See also Matthew 10:29–30.)
God knows everything about me and what I need.

1.B.2. Does God promise to supply what you need or what you want (Matthew 6:19–21)?
He promises to supply what I need.

1.B.3. When does He promise to supply: when you want to have it, or when you need it (Hebrews 4:16)?
God will supply what I need when I need it.

1.C.1. God wants you to **ask** Him to supply what you need (Matthew 6:11; 7:7–11). Why do you think He wants you to do this?
Personal answers will vary.

1.C.2. What does God want you to pursue first, something that is far more important than having material things? (See Matthew 6:32–33.) "Seek first his **kingdom** and his **righteousness**."

1.C.2.a. Who in this world seeks material things first (Matthew 6:32)?
Unbelievers or "pagans" run after material things.

1.C.2.b. Why is it not necessary for you to make pursuing material things your first priority?
God knows what I need and will faithfully meet my needs as I make obeying Him the most important thing in my life.

1.C.2.c. If you put obeying God above meeting your own physical needs, should you worry that you might not have what you need? Why or why not?
God will supply what I need. He knows my physical needs as well as my spiritual needs. He made a promise in Matthew 6:33 to provide for me as I keep my priorities straight.

2.A.1. Read Acts 20:33–35. Jesus said: "It is more blessed to **give** than to **receive**." See also Ephesians 4:28. Why is showing kindness—sharing with those in need—so important for a Christian?
Our giving is more valued in God's sight than what we receive. So God is pleased with our giving and will bless the giver in some way, even when the person receiving does not deserve it.

2.A.2. Can your money help God's kingdom come? How?
Yes. My money can help people experience God's love for them, allow them to hear the gospel, and help teach them how to respond in obedience to Him.

2.A.3. Are you willing to seek God's kingdom first in the way you spend money? In Matthew 6:33, what does God promise if you do?

Personal responses will vary. If I seek God's kingdom first, all the physical things I need will be given to me as well.

2.D.2.a. Paul told the Philippian church that sent money for his needs: "My God will **meet** all your **needs**" (Philippians 4:19).

2.D.2.b. In 2 Corinthians 9:5–15, read Paul's words to the church that had promised a gift for struggling fellow Christians in Jerusalem. Write in your own words the main points Paul was making.
We'll reap as we sow, either generously or sparingly; we should give cheerfully, for this pleases God; God will bless us so we have what we need to do good works; God will enrich us so we can be generous and so that our generosity will result in thanksgiving to God; God's people will be provided for; etc.

2.D.3. God also provides to the giver more for giving to others (2 Corinthians 9:8–11). See verse 8: "have an abundance **for every good deed**" (NASB).

2.D.4. According to 2 Corinthians 9:7, what kind of giver does God love?
God loves a cheerful giver who is happy to give.

Session 9

1.A.1. Read Romans 5:6–8. What did God do to make it possible for you to be forgiven?
Jesus died to pay the penalty for my sins.

1.A.2. God shows His willingness to forgive by loving people even before they ask Him to forgive them. What are some of the ways that He shows love to people who have not asked for forgiveness (Matthew 5:45)?
God shows love by giving them the benefits of sunshine, rain, and many other blessings.

1.A.3. Before Jesus died on the cross to make it possible for every person to be forgiven, how did He show that He is a friend of sinners (Matthew 11:19; Mark 2:13–17)?
Jesus socialized with sinners, healed them, and invited them to follow Him.

1.B.1. God cannot give you His greatest blessings until after you have accepted His forgiveness. What are these greatest blessings (John 3:16–18; Ephesians 2:1–10)?
God rescued me from hell, gave me eternal life, rescues me from slavery to sin, allows me to know Him personally, and prepares me to do good works.

1.B.2. After God initially forgives you, He continues to forgive you when you stumble and sin, are sorry, and ask Him to forgive you (Matthew 6:12; 1 John 1:9). You should ask God to forgive you at least every **day** /week / month (circle one).

2.A.1. So you can be like your **Father in heaven** (Matthew 5:43–48).

2.A.2. Because God has **forgiven** you (Matthew 18:21–35; Ephesians 4:32; Colossians 3:13).

2.B.1. What happens to you (Matthew 6:14–15; Hebrews 12:14–15; Ephesians 4:26–27)?
When I don't forgive others, God doesn't forgive me, I am defiled by bitterness, and I give Satan room to influence me.

2.B.2.   What happens to others around you (Hebrews 12:15)?
          **When I don't forgive others, those around me are defiled by my bitterness as
          they take up my cause or react to attacks or hatred against me.**

Session 10

1.B.2.   When the tempting situation comes, instead of offering any part of yourself to sin
          and becoming a slave to its demands by giving in to temptation, exchange that
          action for the action commanded in Romans 6:13, 16, 19. Summarize what these
          verses teach you to do when tempted.
          **These verses teach me to offer myself to God as His slave, and all parts of my-
          self as instruments to carry out righteous actions.**

2.B.1.   What is your part in this resistance or rescue operation? (See Matthew 6:13;
          Ephesians 6:10–20; James 4:7.)
          **My part is to ask God for help, stand with God's strength against Satan, put
          on God's armor, and pray in the Spirit.**

PoA.1.   What is the promise of 1 John 4:1–4?
          **God is able to expose every demonic influence and teaching and overcome
          their presence and influence.**

PoA.3.c. Tell God you are sorry for your involvement in these things. Then act on James
          4:6–8. The promises here are:
          **God will help the humble and the one who submits to Him and resists (fights
          against) the devil. God will draw near to me if I draw near to Him.**

          The commands are:
          **I must submit to God and resist Satan. I must cleanse my hands (my actions)
          and my heart.**

Session 11

1.A.   Jesus said the communion bread was like His **body** provided for **me** (1 Corinthi-
          ans 11:24).

1.A.1.   Jesus took the bread and **broke** it for the disciples to eat. This was symbolic of the
          breaking of His body in death to give life to those who would "eat" (John 6:51).

1.A.2.a. A person must "take" or receive **Jesus** to have eternal life (John 1:12).

1.B.1.   The cup of wine is a reminder that Jesus was crushed to release His life-purchas-
          ing blood. In what ways would wine be an appropriate symbol of Jesus' blood?
          **Wine is the lifeblood of the grape that must be crushed (lose its life) to release
          it so people can receive its nourishment and refreshing.**

1.C.1.   As you share or have communion with Jesus at the Lord's Supper, what should
          you be thinking about besides Jesus (Matthew 26:29; 1 Corinthians 11:26)?
          **I should be thinking about Jesus' coming back to earth and about eating and
          drinking with Jesus in His Father's kingdom.**

1.C.2.   Read John 14:3; 1 Thessalonians 4:13–18; and 1 Corinthians 15:50–53. How and
          in what condition will we arrive at the place Jesus has prepared for us?

Jesus will come back to get us, and we will meet Him in the air to live with Him forever in new eternal bodies.

2.A.1.   The Bible says a person may be eating the bread and drinking the cup of the Lord in an unworthy manner (1 Corinthians 11:27). Note: The emphasis here is on the right manner or way in which a person should eat and drink—not on the person's worthiness of this privilege. The word **worthy** in the original language means "fitting" or "appropriate.") Why is it wrong for a person to eat and drink in an unworthy manner? (Look again at 1 Corinthians 11:27.)
Whoever eats the bread or drinks the cup of the Lord in an unworthy manner is actually insulting Christ by demeaning or not taking seriously the sacredness and significance of His death for us.

2.A.2.   Why would it not be right for an unbeliever to take part in this communion observance?
It would be dishonest and dishonoring to Jesus because the unbeliever has not accepted Jesus as the source of his or her life and enjoys no communion with the Lord.

2.B.1.   Some of the Corinthian believers were coming for the Lord's Supper but not thinking of the Lord (verse 20) or the other members of His body who had come to worship with them (verses 22, 29). From 1 Corinthians 11:21, 34, what does it seem they were thinking of instead?
It seems these people were thinking of their own hunger rather than of other believers or of the Lord.

2.B.2.   How serious was their offense in God's eyes (1 Corinthians 11:27)?
This was a serious insult to God.

2.B.3.   God's "judgment" was not to reject them. What did God allow to happen to them, and for what reason? 1 Corinthians 11:30, 32:
God allowed weakness, sickness and death to discipline them, causing them to seek God in their distress rather than drifting away from God in their sin.

God's discipline should help us correct our behavior, which will then help us avoid the dangers of continuing in sin. Do you examine your own heart and life each day to see if there are things in you that are displeasing to God?

Personal responses will vary.

2.C.1.   How can you avoid being disciplined by God (1 Corinthians 11:31)?
I can avoid discipline by evaluating myself on my own initiative.

2.C.2.   What then should you do before sharing in the Lord's Supper (1 Corinthians 11:28, 31)?
I should examine and evaluate my relationship with God and repent of or correct any sin I find in my life.

2.C.3.   When you examine yourself and discover some sin of thought or action, what should you do before taking part in the Lord's Supper? (See 1 John 1:9.)
I should ask God to forgive me and commit myself to specific action that the Spirit shows me to do to correct my actions.

2.C.4.   Should you examine yourself only before taking part in the Lord's Supper? Why or why not?
No, I should examine myself more frequently, because self-awareness is vital to growing in God and holy living.

Session 12

2.A.3.   Now consider the Holy Spirit's role in Jesus' life as described in Luke 4:18–19 and Acts 10:38. What or Who was flowing out of Jesus?
God's love was flowing out of Jesus in spiritual power. The Holy Spirit was flowing out of Jesus.

2.B.1.   According to Romans 5:5, from where does this fruit come?
This fruit comes from the Holy Spirit and God's love.

2.B.2.   Make a list from Galatians 5:22–23. "The fruit of the Spirit is…"
"…love, joy, peace, patience, kindness, goodness, faithfulness, gentleness, and self-control."

2.B.5.   In John 21:15–19, Jesus explained to Peter how to obey the top two commands to function as a pastor. In what ways did Peter need the fruit of the Spirit to accomplish what Jesus was saying he should do?
Peter needs the character traits that are spiritual fruit to effectively care for Jesus' sheep with the right attitudes and motivation.

3.A.1.   Identify the two opponents squaring off against each other in Romans 5:17.
The two battling for control in your life are the sinful nature or flesh and the Holy Spirit.

3.A.2.   You pick the winner of each battle by giving in to the desire of your **flesh** or by turning to the **Holy Spirit** to help you act His way.

3.B.1.   Pray every morning guided by Galatians 5:16, 22–25. Write down the guidelines for praying that you see in this passage.
(1) Let the Spirit guide me today instead of trying to guide myself;
(2) Let me show and experience each fruit of the Spirit today with my family, my coworkers, my boss, etc.

3.C.1.a.   Verse 11: Consider yourself to be **dead** to sin, which makes it possible for you to do as described in verse 13.

3.C.1.b.   Verse 13: What does this verse give as the action that is the alternative to being dead to sin?
Then, "present yourselves to God as those alive from the dead [ready for action], and your members as instruments [tools] of righteousness to God" (Romans 6:13).

3.C.2.a.   First, remember that you are considering yourself to be **alive** to God and **dead** to sin (Romans 6:11–12).

3.C.2.b.   Then, follow verse 13 and present yourself to God to receive instruction as to what to do next instead of doing what your natural self is urging you to do. All the members of your body are alive from the dead (ready for action), and are ready to be instruments or tools of **righteousness or to do what is right** as directed by God (Romans 6:13).

Example: When you are angry, you should turn away from the temptation to react in anger and instead present yourself to God to release the Spirit-fruit or fruits of _____ to operate instead of anger.

Just find one or more fruit of the Spirit that would be a God-pleasing replacement for anger, and ask the Spirit to activate that instead of anger.

PoA.2a. Eyes that see needs. According to Matthew 9:36, what need did Jesus see?
He saw crowds of people, harassed and helpless, like sheep without a shepherd.

PoA.2.b. Real concern for people with needs. In Matthew 9:36, how do you know Jesus was concerned for the people?
Jesus felt compassion for them because of their needs and separation from Him.

Psalm 126:5–6: "He that sows in tears shall reap with joy." Acts 20:31: "I did not cease to admonish each one with **tears**."

Acts 20:31: What did Paul have plenty of as he cared for people?
Paul had plenty of tears.

Session 13

1.A.1. Luke 4:18: "The **Spirit** of the Lord is **on** or **upon** me, because he has anointed me."

1.A.2. Acts 10:38: "God anointed Jesus of Nazareth with the **Holy Spirit** and **power**, and…he went around doing good and healing…because God was with him."

1.B.1. What did Jesus tell them to wait for (Acts 1:4–5)?
He told them to wait for what the Father had promised—the baptism in the Holy Spirit.

1.B.2. Who would baptize them in the Holy Spirit (John 1:33–34)?
Jesus would be the baptizer.

1.B.3.a. What would happen. (Describe it here.)
The disciples would receive power after the Holy Spirit came on them.

1.B.3.b. What they would become. (Summarize it here.)
The empowered disciples would become witnesses for Jesus.

1.B.3.c. Where they would do this. (Define their mission field here.)
The disciples would take the good news to Jerusalem, all Judea and Samaria, and to the ends of the earth—everywhere!

1.B.4. According to Luke 24:49–53 and Acts 1:13–14, what did the disciples do in Jerusalem?
The disciples stayed in the temple praising God and continued in united prayer.

1.C.1. Read Acts 2:4, 6, 11, 14–18, 36–41. What did the Holy Spirit do through people and in people on the Day of Pentecost?

The Holy Spirit helped them speak in languages they didn't know, declaring the wonders of God. Peter preached with great power and courage. Three thousand Jews believed and accepted Jesus as Messiah.

1.C.2. Read Jesus' promise in Mark 1:16–18: "I will make you **fishers** of men." How does Acts 4:31 show this happening?
Believers spoke the gospel message with boldness in spite of danger.

1.C.3.a. Describe Peter before he was filled with the Spirit (John 13:36–38; 18:1–27).
Peter said he would be totally loyal to Jesus, but he slept through the time Jesus asked him to pray. He acted independently and denied Jesus out of fear.

1.C.3.b. Describe Peter after he was filled with the Spirit (Acts 4:13; 5:17–32). What can you tell about Peter's change of character by what he wrote in 1 Peter 3:8–17?
After he was filled with the Spirit, Peter was bold, courageous, a relentless witness, gentle, kind, forgiving, self-controlled, full of faith, dependent on the Spirit, and humble.

1.C.4.1. According to Acts 2:39, who does God want to have this experience of being filled with the Spirit?
This experience is for every Christian.

2.A.1. Jesus wants you to receive power so that you can be what? (Read Acts 1:8.) Do you want more power—the ability—to tell other people about Jesus?
The power of the Holy Spirit helps me to be a witness. Personal responses will vary.

Session 14

1.Sum.1. **Receive** God's love through **Jesus Christ**.

1.Sum.2. **Respond** to God with **love and worship**.

1.Sum.3. **Release** God's love through **you to other people**.

2.Sum. **Ask** forgiveness from Jesus, your **sacrifice** (sin payment).

Believe in Jesus as your living **Savior** (helping friend).

Cooperate each day with Jesus as your **Lord** (leader).

Concl. Write in the missing words from John 14:16. Jesus said, "I am the **way**, the **truth**, and the **life**. No one **comes** to the Father [God], except **through** me." Do you understand what Jesus said well enough to be able to explain it to someone else?

Personal answers will vary.

Session 15

2.C.1.a. Who does Jesus make responsible for a new believer's baptism in water (Matthew 28:19)?
The Christian who is discipling the new believer and the new believer are both responsible.

2.C.2.a. Water baptism is a (circle one) suggestion / **command** for both the church family and the new believer (Mark 16:16; Acts 2:38).

3.B.2.a. For words that are **clear and seasoned with grace**. (Colossians 4:3–4, 6).

3.B.2.b. For conduct that is **wise** (Colossians 4:5).

3.B.2.c. For a manner that is **bold** (Ephesians 6:19–20).

3.B.3. For an open door for witness (Colossians 4:3).

3.B.4. For God's help in **making the most of the opportunity** (Colossians 4:5).

PoA.1. Have you been sent by the Lord of the Harvest?
Yes.

PoA.1.a. To whom?
I am to go to the lost people in my life, especially…(give names).

PoA.1.b. To do what?
I am to tell them the good news, lead them to Jesus, and disciple them to disciple others.

Made in the USA
Las Vegas, NV
16 September 2023

77667067R00103